I0522009

# POWER
## OF *truth*

*Overcoming 25 Years of Darkness*

A True Cult Survivor Story

———————➤✸◄———————

Anna Armstrong

Copyright 2023 by Anna Armstrong. All Rights Reserved.

No part of this book may be reproduced or transmitted in any form or by any means, electronic or mechanical, including photocopying and recording, or by any information storage and retrieval system, without permission in writing from the author and publisher.

Unless otherwise noted, Scripture quotations are taken from the Holy Bible, New International Version, Zondervan Publishing House, 1984

Printed in the United States of America
2023 First Edition
10 9 8 7 6 5 4 3 2 1

Subject Index:
Anna
Title: Power of Truth. Overcoming 25 Years of Darkness. A True
        Cult Survivor Story
1. Religious Cults 2. Self-help 3. Empowerment 4. Christian
    Inspiration 5. Memoir 6. Hassan Bite Model
Paperback: 979-8-9894911-1-7
Library of Congress Card Catalog Number: 2023922143


Website: poweroftruthbook.com

# Praise for Power of Truth...

"This book by Anna Armstrong is one that mesmerizes the person reading it. I was drawn right in from the very beginning as if I myself was Anna Armstrong struggling to be loved and accepted.

In Chapter 10, under the heading "Backstabbing and Backbiting," I was struck by the words. Basically, if you're "right" with Daddy Leviathan, then you're right with God. Any disagreement with Daddy Leviathan about his lifestyle meant that your soul was in danger.

It made me quite sad to know that this kind of total mind control and manipulation happened to Anna and that this happens today under the guise of serving God.

This book is a "Must Read" for anyone who is now or has ever been in a cult."

*Bishop Michael V. Robinson*
*New York, NY*

# Dedication

To The Bishop because without him, I would not be living my best days today. Also, to all members, past and present, of The Group whom I love dearly and hope this book brings them deliverance into a better life.

# Acknowledgments

I want to thank my husband because, without him, I would not have accomplished this work. He bore my pain, my laughter, my joys, and my tears. He is my rock, and I am so grateful that God brought him back into my life. I also want to thank all of my family. I thank my departed loved ones and my siblings, cousins, nieces, and nephews: Thank You for allowing me to come back into the family after being away for over 20 years. To my ghostwriter, you are a true warrior of God. I thank you for bearing me up when the writing got difficult. I didn't plan it, but you bore some of my pain and provided me with the comfort that God gave to you. Thank you, Bishop Robinson, for allowing God to position you into my life after the passing of my beloved Bishop. To the family of The Bishop, his wife, and children: thank you for embracing me as part of your family. Thank you to my therapists, the unspoken occupational heroes, and the she-roes who helped me understand how the mind works.

# TABLE OF CONTENTS

Dedication ........................................................................ iv

Acknowledgments .......................................................... v

Author's Note: ................................................................ xi

Introduction .................................................................... 1

**Part I: My Early Years** ............................................**5**

Chapter 1: Isn't She Lovely .......................................... 7

Chapter 2: The Preacher Man ...................................... 12

Chapter 3: Connecting The Dots .................................. 16

      Young Disciples ..................................................... 21

Chapter 4: Father Figure .............................................. 23

      A Budding Artist ................................................... 25

Chapter 5: Following The Crowd ................................. 27

**Part II: My Feeding Stage** .....................................**31**

Chapter 6: Teenage Love .............................................. 33

Chapter 7: Finding My Stride ...................................... 35

Chapter 8: Ivy Leaguer ................................................. 41

      Keep Running ........................................................ 42

      Perfection................................................................ 45

Chapter 9: Daddy Leviathan: The False Prophet ............ 49

A Perverted Prophet ................................................ 50

A Woman Scorned .................................................. 53

Lust, Hedonism, And Lies ....................................... 57

Chapter 10: Grooming ............................................... 59

A Close Watch ....................................................... 63

Guadeloupe............................................................ 63

Backstabbing And Backbiting ................................ 66

Chapter 11: True Love Blockers ................................. 69

Chapter 12: Music For The Soul................................. 74

Rough Riders ......................................................... 80

Chapter 13: Forsake All Others ................................. 81

Chapter 14: The Illness Of My Pain........................... 87

Marvella's Diffraction............................................. 89

Another Kick In The Gut ........................................ 90

Chapter 15: The Ostracized Wife ............................... 93

Searching For Enlightenment.................................. 95

Forbidden Videos................................................... 97

The Chosen Wife .................................................... 99

Sewing His Royal Oats ........................................... 101

Plans To Leave ....................................................... 103

Chapter 16: The Clean-Up Woman ............................ 109

The Queen Mother ................................................. 110

Lies And Confrontation ......................................... 116

Hell Nights............................................................ 117

Idol Worship.......................................................... 125

Chapter 17: The Elite And Imps................................. 127

Elder Lela, The Forgotten Wife .............................. 127

Elder Lulu ............................................................. 129

If It Acts Like A Snake… ........................................ 130

Chapter 18: Give Good Measure.................................................. 135

## Part III: My Transition.................................................**145**

Chapter 19: Ghana Trip 2010.................................................. 147
    Ghana Trip 2011 ........................................................ 149
    The Great I Am ........................................................ 152
    Summer Of 2012 ...................................................... 155

Chapter 20: A New Attitude.................................................. 156

Chapter 21: My Forever Sister............................................... 159
    The Funeral .............................................................. 161

Chapter 22: Hurricane Sandy ............................................... 162

Chapter 23: Brothers Betrayed ............................................. 167
    Sexual Healing........................................................... 171
    A Special Visitor ....................................................... 172
    Broke, Broken & Renewed ..................................... 173

Chapter 24: A Sister Betrayed............................................... 176
    The Writing On The Wall........................................ 179

## Part IV: Metamorphosis Adult Butterfly: .............................**185**

Chapter 25: A True Spiritual Father ..................................... 187
    What Life I Have Left... ........................................... 192
    Snowy Day Of Revelation........................................ 193

Chapter 26: Freedom Wings ................................................. 198
    Prelude To My Boaz ................................................ 199

Epilogue................................................................................. 205

My 12 Steps To Loving Me .................................................. 207

Cult Tactics............................................................................ 208

Influence Continuum Chart.................................................209

BITE Model Charts...............................................................210

About The Author: ...............................................................215

## Organizational Charts of The Group

The Beginnings House of MOTS .................................................48, 195

The Group Cult Formation ...................................................................66

## Family Incest Trees

Shirley & Birdie (Sisters) ........................................................................84

Lela and Lulu (Twins) .............................................................................85

Afro-American Family in Ghana .........................................................151

## The Group's International Caste

System as of 2012..................................................................................155

American Family in Ghana...................................................................166

# AUTHOR'S NOTE:

This nonfiction work depicts actual events in my life and is told as truthfully as I remember. While all the stories in this book are true, some names and identifying details have been changed to protect the privacy of the people involved.

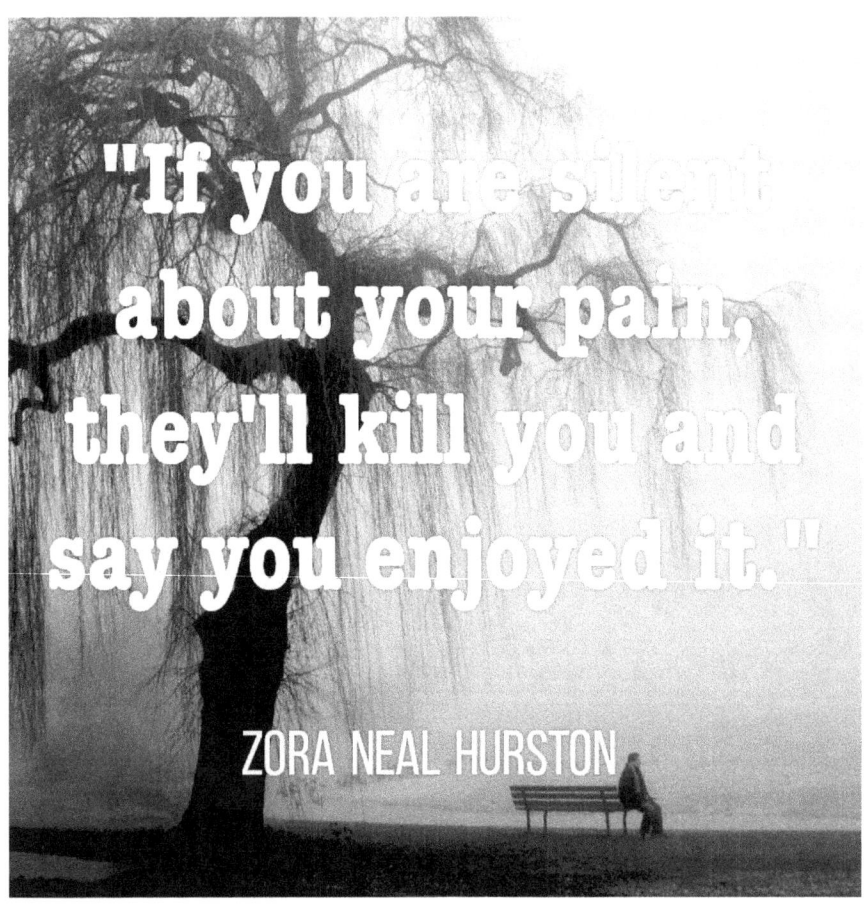

"If you are silent about your pain, they'll kill you and say you enjoyed it."

ZORA NEAL HURSTON

# INTRODUCTION

*"The most common way people give up their power is by
thinking they don't have any."*
**Alice Walker**

Have you ever heard of Dr. Masaru Emoto's experiment with two glasses of water? Although there are a few variations to this experiment, the results are the same. One glass of water was placed in a room, and a group was told to think only good thoughts and to speak positively towards the glass. The first glass was removed and replaced with another glass of water, and the same group was instructed to think only negative thoughts and speak dreadful words about the glass. Both glasses were stored in the same controlled environment. After several days, the first glass of water appeared fresh and clear. However, the second glass developed mold and a stench.

Although there are differing opinions as to the validity of this exercise, as a scientist, I equate some truth to this experiment. Since more than half of our bodies are composed of water, we can be impacted by outside factors such as negative or positive words, visuals, and environments. If we are placed in an environment where everyone speaks unfavorably towards us or exerts harsh judgments directed at us, then we will eventually believe that those words and actions are justified and true. Yet if we are nurtured and spoken to with encouraging words and shown integrity and concrete examples of what is good, we will be empowered to achieve great things. I've learned that daily positive affirmations are a lifeline to better mental and physical health.

I survived a Christian-themed cult for 25 years that primarily operated out of New Jersey and Ghana, West Africa, with origins of being on college campuses throughout the northeast. I was heavily recruited as a first-year college student at an Ivy League University. During that time, I was lost and unsure of my future. I had no idea I was operating at an alarmingly low self-esteem, despite being a college track and field record holder with a GPA over 3.0.

As a member of this apparently thriving "saints living free from sin" cult ("The Group"), I was constantly scolded, shunned, ridiculed, and looked down upon, despite being one of the primary financial providers helping The Group to grow and prosper for over two decades. No matter how hard I tried to respect the Elders, humble myself, zip up my smart mouth, and forsake my family and friends, I would never be taught and have the opportunity to elevate into the "Elite class." To add to my misery, I was told I would never attain the required spiritual growth or honor as a spiritual leader in The Group's ministry. "This is as good as she'll get," the Leader boasted one day.

The Group sprung out of a humble church in Elizabeth, New Jersey. The first Pastor was a God-fearing, well-known woman recognized for her strength and power as a prayer warrior. Most parishioners affectionately called her "Ma." Years later, her children, their spouses, and some followers split from Ma's true biblical teaching. They began to manipulate God's word and His people to elevate themselves as king and queens over the flock.

Ma's offspring were skilled at teaching and delivering the word of God, yet their spouses interspersed it with lust, lies, adultery, and greed. This "splitting" birthed a godforsaken Group that made an adulterous, greedy, manipulative man the highest leader and prophet of The Group. Throughout this book, I call the leader Daddy Leviathan, a reference in the Old Testament as, a huge, evil sea monster. Daddy Leviathan can also mean something enormous, which is definitely true of his powerful presence and obesity.

Four Elders of The Group were controlling me. Each one had a way of manipulating and twisting God's Word for their personal gain.

Members of The Group worshipped the Elders as if they were Gods. We were told that the Elders were free from sin. The order of authority in The Group was that Daddy Leviathan was number one. Then whenever Daddy Leviathan was not around, his number two henchwoman, Shirley, was front and center pumping him up. She would adamantly chastise us and say, "He's a prophet of God, and if you go against the word of the prophet, that means you're going against God!"

Daddy Leviathan was fully aware of Shirley's tactics, and in hindsight, their act was so rehearsed. Her role was to set the stage for the culture by continuing to reinforce that all of the followers had to be in alignment with him and believe every single word from his mouth. If anyone ever questioned him or thought ill-will towards him, we would be openly scolded, mocked, and left out to dry in front of the others.

The other two Elders were twin sisters, Lulu and Lela. Lela was Daddy Leviathan's legal wife, although, throughout my time there, he acquired several other wives and children. And yes, nearly every woman in The Group had sexual relations with Daddy Leviathan. My sexual encounters occurred just a few times early on, and afterward, I was designated a "spiritual wife." This label meant that I was doomed to a future as an unwilling type of nun, banned from having a legal husband and my own family. I was regarded as a left-over woman rejected by the prophet and never to be touched again by him, but never belong to anyone else.

The Elders told me early on that I was not gifted in preaching or teaching, so I could never be in an instructional class to hone my gifts. I was not accepted by anyone. I was talked about and ridiculed often. I was even chastised for calling myself a servant by the Elders. After all, I was cleaning bathrooms, doing chores, and helping out at the children's school. I was always a bit shy and did not speak confidently. Everyone around me had an alluring stage presence and charisma and used flowery words. I stood out like a sore thumb, yet I was eager to learn and desperately wanted to take the Gospel to the world.

The dichotomy of it all is that I was living a double life. I was a superhero and team leader for a Fortune 100 pharmaceutical company at work. Yet when I left the office, I was a mere pheasant and slept on the floor of the cult leader in a home with his family and pseudo-wives. Despite all of this, I excelled in my career for many years, getting promotions and a six-figure salary. The more money I made, the more I gave to the Group.

*"The way to right wrongs is to turn the truth upon them."*
**Ida B. Wells**

I am not writing this book to bash Christianity. Instead, I am documenting my 26-year experience in a cult that successfully used Christianity as a tool to condemn and hold people captive in their minds. Some of the victims who have escaped over the years have gone on to live normal lives, but past memories still haunt some. It all depends on how deep you were in the cult while you were there. I was deep enough to know many of the dirty secrets that went on behind closed doors outside of the boundaries of the Bible studies that went on every night for many years. Although I was told the secret of secrets, I was still deemed as the least among the Elders and other leaders and treated as such. I know all of the leaders never thought that I would leave. "Surely, she cannot survive without us. She would surely lose her mind," is what was drilled into me the entire time I was under their grasp. But thank God He sent a greater power that saved me from their grip, the *Power of Truth*!

As a survivor of The Group, I believe my growth and transformation are like the four-stage metamorphosis of the butterfly: egg, larva (caterpillar), pupa (transition), and adult (butterfly). It was not an easy process, and it took several years of selfless dedication to an evil, conflicting, corrupt, false religious sham. The transition stage of the pupa is a stage where the creature is not even recognized: it is in a soupy, liquid state. For most of the time during my stay in The Group, I didn't know who I was, looking for a face to wear, but I was unrecognizable even to myself. But I thank my God that I have come out stronger.

My prayer for those reading this book is for you to love yourself first and foremost. By doing so, you will have the ability to ward off the negative energy from others that would seek to control you. Unconditional love requires no help from any man or woman. The power to control your destiny is within you. Don't ever let anyone take that away from you.

# PART I
# My Early Years

*The Egg: Female butterflies lay very small eggs on plants*

*"Before I formed you in the womb, I knew you…"*
**Jeremiah 1:5 (NIV)**

# CHAPTER 1

# Isn't She Lovely

*"A baby is God's opinion that life should go on."*
**Carl Sandburg**

I was born at Mount Sinai Hospital in New York City. My mother was close to 40 years old when she had me. Mom worked as a telephone switchboard operator at the New York Telephone Company for about three years. Then one day, while working the switchboard, connecting people's calls, she felt a big kick in her belly. She didn't know she was five months pregnant with me! Mom got fired from her job because she was pregnant. Nevertheless, my birth was an unexpected pleasant surprise. Due to complications from her previous delivery, the doctors advised her to have a cesarean section.

Mom said she would never forget the contrasting experience between my birth and my brother before me. He was born into this world in strangulation with his umbilical cord tied around his neck, losing oxygen to his brain, which has led to a lifelong learning disability. To this day, I feel my brother was a sacrifice for me. His difficult entrance into this world caused the doctors to recommend a cesarean section when it came time for my arrival. This allowed mom to have her easiest and most pleasant birthing experience, and in contrast to my brother, I was born with exceptional learning abilities that showed up in my late high school and college years.

My mom recalled that she went to the hospital early and was treated very nicely. They fed her great food, "soup to nuts," as she always said! She was treated like a Queen. Then when I was born, she said I was the most beautiful baby she had ever seen. She recalled that all the nurses on the floor could not put me down because I was the loveliest baby. Every time she told me this, I always said to myself, *Oh, she is just saying that because that's how moms feel about their babies*. However, throughout my life, I would get compliments on my beauty often. I didn't really allow it to sink in and feel good about myself until many years later.

I believe that now I am living in the beauty that God planned for me from the very beginning. Beauty that starts deep, deep in the soul, and exudes through the body and into the aura that surrounds me. My inner beauty seeks to be a blessing to anyone that comes into my presence. This is spiritual beauty that can be attained by anyone that has loved from above and desires to spread their love by being an example, not by ramming words and Scriptures down people's throats.

My mom went to church every Sunday, but I didn't consider her a spiritual person for many years. Growing up at home, she never openly prayed or read the Bible. Mom was the youngest of 12 children, and her father died when she was two years old. Her family was split up, and she was raised from sibling to sibling, so she did not have anyone to guide her in life. As I matured, I realized that she could not give me what she never had.

********

As a young woman, my mother was very beautiful. Redbone skin, high cheekbones, and a million-dollar smile. She was a petite girl with an hourglass figure. Mom was starry-eyed and wanted a house with children to fill it. She was a dedicated mother and worker. She worked part-time at Macy's Herald Square to ensure she was present when we got home from school. She also took the summers off while we were out of school. Her pride and joy in life were her children, and up to her last days, she always told me how proud she was of all of us.

Mom was also an accomplished singer who took singing lessons at Carnegie Hall and sang on the local radio with her friends when she was young. Singing was the core foundation of who my mom was. It was something that she was born to do, handed down from my praying grandmother, who was a church evangelist. Grandma not only sang, but she taught herself to play multiple instruments, including the piano and horns. Even as a senior citizen in her 90s, and despite blindness, inability to walk, and increasing state of dementia, Mom was still very beautiful to gaze upon and had the most beautiful voice.

My father was a tall, statuesque, handsome man with a full beard, brown-skinned, and a voice deeper than James Earl Jones. His deep voice would make Darth Vader run for cover! I don't know much about my Dad's family, but I do know his mother was Native American and lived on a reservation in upstate New York. Mom told me Dad's mother was beautiful with hair down to her waist, but she had a mean side. I was told she poured hot grease on my father's dad, and that story resonates with me. To this day, I believe my father may have experienced abuse growing up.

My parents met through other friends. They were pen pals when my dad was in the military. Once he left the military, they married and lived in a one-room apartment in Brooklyn. Initially, my father had a good job as a police officer. But then, suddenly, he was fired. My brother told me Dad was treated unfairly after he had to use his club to put someone in their place. Being a black man with a blue-collar job in the 1960s was very difficult to survive because of racism, and macro and microaggressions, to say the least. As time went on, Dad couldn't seem to hold down a steady job for long. All the while, as the number of mouths to feed increased, so did the tension between my parents.

By the time I was born, my parents had been together for 15 years. At that time, they had moved into an apartment complex in Woodside, New York. The three bedrooms were filled with all five children: three brothers, and one sister, with me being the youngest. Although we were only together as a family for the first five years of my life, I have vivid memories of those years, and they are so precious to me.

I remember when my siblings and I gathered for a family photo when I was no more than a year old, and the photographer said, "Now everybody say cheese!'" And then he snapped the photo. Right at that moment in my mind, I said, *What is cheese?* Every time I see that family photo, I laugh because all of my siblings had big "cheesy" smiles, and I have a glazed look on my face!

I also remember my mother giving me a bath in the kitchen sink as a baby. I remember being in the water in the steel kitchen sink and looking into my mom's face, and seeing her smiling back at me. Even then, I knew and felt my mom loved me very, very much. During those early childhood days, I wore leg braces because I was extremely pigeon-toed. I remember the times that I slept with Mom and Dad, and years later, Mom used to joke about me hitting both of them in the head with my legs during the night. I was given the offer by the doctors to have my ankles broken and reset to fix my feet, but at five years old, my parents allowed me to make the first major decision in my life. I opted not to have the surgery, and they respected my decision.

For the first five years of my life, our home was always alive and active with laughter and fun. My big brother Brandon had more than one hundred toy soldiers that he would spend hours playing with. This was a precursor to his long military career in the Army. My big brother Robert always told jokes, making us laugh with his "burp talking." He was an avid reader of comic books, whose collection I picked up and read many years later. He was also an excellent artist and piano player. My sister had a very strong personality and kept me in line around the house as I ran around with my little blue blanket sucking my thumb. And Timmy, my brother closest to me in age, was four years older than me. Timmy did not speak a word until he was 12 years old. If he made a noise with his voice, it was always celebrated.

I remember a lot of good times. Even though we did not have much materially, we had each other, and we were well taken care of. However, there was one early memory that was not good. And looking back, I realize there were things happening between Mom and Dad before I came onto the scene.

One day as I was lying on the bed in Mom and Dad's room, I remember playing with my little feet. My mother and father were at the edge of the bed, having a discussion. Then it happened. Something I will never ever forget. Daddy slapped Mommy so hard. It was the loudest noise I had ever heard. Mom fell on the bed next to me with her hands covering her face for what seemed like a long time. I could feel that she was in great physical pain. I didn't understand what was happening, but I know it was the first imprint of accepting abuse from a male figure. Years later, Mommy told me that my daddy knocked all of the teeth out of her mouth. I never mentioned to her that I remember being present during that incident. So, from the late 1960s to her last days, my Mom wore dentures because of that single powerful slap in the face. For years, I often wondered, *Why on earth would he hurt her like that*?

# CHAPTER 2

# The Preacher Man

*"...But one thing daddy sure could do right*
*He could swear, Oh, lord, I declare..."*
**Gladys Knight & the Pips**

During those first five years of my life, I remember dreaming that I saw my father as a giant god in the clouds flying with his arms out like a cross, I guess because he had such spiritual authority in the home. We all reverenced Daddy, and he was highly revered in the spiritual community.

Despite his shortcomings, I love my father. I respect the fact that he was known to be a prophet and, for a long time, only spoke and lived by the word of God, the Holy Bible. He has many witnesses that, for many years until he diverted in the faith, everything he said would happen came to pass. He always emphasized to his followers that if any man makes claims, they must be backed up by the written word of God. Dad was skilled in the Scriptures and was self-taught in the ancient Greek language so that he could understand the New Testament Scriptures closer to their truer form.

He taught much about God's coming judgment, and his audience was the church itself, warning them to speak, teach and live the truth. Dad was a contemporary of Malcolm X. He participated in the verbal sparring between community leaders where history, religion, and social justice topics were hotly debated at House's Barbershop in Harlem. Malcolm X's mosque was nearby, and other religious leaders in the community, along with my dad, would go to House's Barbershop and "spar" about the important issues of the time while getting their fresh, clean grooming.

Dad was an eloquent and powerful speaker with a giant-sized presence. Because of his powerful and skillful teachings, and the giant-sized presence of God, he gained a following of believers that had the utmost confidence in him, following faithfully. He never required lots of money, fancy clothes, or cars. After the divorce, I got to meet Dad in a very humbled state, living in Harlem with meager amenities. He was a gifted spiritual teacher that never asked anyone for anything but instead found ways to give to folks in need. By the time I got to know him as an adult, he had gone through a season of change, diverting from the Scriptures.

As Dad delved deeper into religion and entered into a change of doctrine, he began acting strange and paranoid. Mom told me years later that he used to write her notes saying, "Susan will die" and "Susan is Satan." How ironic it is that my mother, who lived well into her 90s, outlived my father by over 25 years!

Aside from the slapping incident etched in my memory, I don't recall other incidents of violence or abuse until the night Daddy walked out on us. That night there was a lot of yelling and arguing, and my brother Timmy and I were on the couch crying. My father stormed into the room and started slapping us hard on the legs, which made us scream and cry more. I was crying because my father was beating us for no reason—not because of the actual stinging pain against my bare legs.

My mother ran over to stop him from beating us, and he turned around and wrapped his huge hands over her tiny neck, and began to choke her. He had the most frustrating look on his face, and I saw some of her life force leave her face. She was dying. Thank God my two brothers ran over, and their united efforts were strong enough to pull him off. My mom fell to the floor, gasping for air, and my father headed straight for the door. Mom pulled herself together on the floor and raised one arm towards him, and let out a pained, loud cry, "Don't leave!" as he slammed the door behind him. Mom held her head down and cried over and over "20 years! 20 years!" She was devastated and although I was only a five years old toddler, I could feel her pain.

Hence, this was my second image of accepting abuse from a male figure. I witnessed this holy man of God leave his entire family and continue to work as a full-time minister out of his Harlem apartment. He left Mommy to feed five mouths on her own. She was devastated. All of us were forever stung by the pain of separation between the two people we loved so much.

I was too young to reflect on the irony of my father's religiosity and the contradiction of leaving your family. Looking back, how could he justify leaving us if he was a man of the cloth? I know that Mom was not the easiest person to be with, but it doesn't give anyone the right to strike another person. At that time, we were still living in an apartment in the Woodside area of Queens, New York. Dad moved to a very poor section of Harlem. The happy aura of the home with my siblings quickly declined. My big brother went away to the army, and mom became a single parent with neighbors helping to watch me because she had to find a job and start working to support us.

As time went on, my dad took the bus from Harlem to meet my brother and me at a local McDonald's. Other times, we went to visit him in Harlem, and he would pray over us fervently with tears streaming down his face, calling out to God, "Father God protect my children. Lord, you promised me that all my children would be saved. So please, Father, protect these two."

When my brother and I got older, the visits with my dad were sporadic, and I don't recall seeing him much during high school. I did visit him once or twice when I was at junior college in Farmingdale. As the youngest, I had a deep bond with both of my parents. His leaving left a huge void in my life. So many times, I wanted to ask him, "Why did you leave us?" "Why didn't you teach me about life?" "Why didn't you allow me the benefit of the wisdom of a father?"

Although I wanted him badly in my life, I cherished the moments I got to spend with him. My favorite time was when I was living in Farmingdale, and I met up with him in Harlem. My father had a powerful presence, and I always felt he was a great man of God, but there was bitterness about how he felt about my mom. He had this bitterness about him most of the time I visited him. However, on his deathbed, he said he wished her and my stepfather the best, praying for their salvation with a sincere heart.

When Dad was 61 years old, he was hospitalized in Columbus Hospital with brain cancer. For the first time, I saw that he had a change of heart toward Mom. He died on Thanksgiving Day, 1992. I saw him the day before, and I spoke to him an hour before he died. Dad was full of thanksgiving, despite his fight with cancer. My brother Robert was there with my dad when he died. He was my dad's spiritual apprentice for a couple of years, and they were very close.

Prior to his death, I spoke to him a few times when I joined The Group. He had a bad feeling about The Group, and he did not like them. One time He spoke to Shirley on the phone. My father had a sharp tongue, and he spoke his mind. I don't know what the conversation was about, but he warned me they were keeping me in the back and not in the front, where I belonged. He must have seen my future and could not understand how I could advance and grow with a group like theirs.

# CHAPTER 3

# Connecting The Dots

*"Yes, Mother. I can see that you are flawed. You have not hidden it. That is your greatest gift to me."*
**Alice Walker**

Two years had passed since Mom and Dad split, and we were still in the apartment in Woodside, minus Brandon, my oldest brother. Mom had been working a lot but did save funds to treat herself to a getaway trip to Aruba, sponsored by a club in Queens, where her brother was a member. Mom was making new friends and finding ways to move on with her life. I came home from school one day, and Mom was packing up casually, saying, "Anna, we're moving today."

I did not know how to process what she said. We got into a truck with a man I had never seen before. Mom did not prepare me by explaining to me that she got married to this man, nor do I remember the introductions. This was the strangest day of my life at this point, and moving was even stranger.

When I arrived at my new elementary school, I was challenged by a mean girl to a fight in my first week. Prior to that, fighting was foreign to me—it didn't make any sense. The girl and her friends waited for me outside and surrounded me. She swung at me, and in defense, I threw her up against the brick wall by accident. She hit her head and ran off. Luckily, none of the other girls challenged me again. Yet the boys did much worse.

Since I was the new girl in school, I was also targeted by this posse of bad boys. The lunchtime bell rang, and it was time for recess. I was out enjoying myself on the swing. I was going to jump off, but instead, this boy jumped on me while swinging and began to hump on me. We fell off the swing, and his friends held me down to the ground and grabbed my arms and legs. The boy tried to take my panties off and penetrate me. Thank God I had on my leotards for dance class, and he couldn't get my tights and panties off. So, he decided to mimic the sex act on top of me while his friends held me down. I was screaming and crying. Finally, a teacher ran to help me and threw the boy off me.

The school brought my mom in, and they questioned if there was penetration. I could sense that my mom was sad and hurt by what happened to me, but she was also ashamed, so she did not want to talk about it afterward. Since there was no penetration, that was the end of the interrogation. No harm, no foul, according to the grown-ups. It was a huge burden to carry as a seven-year-old. The school did not offer counseling or any follow-up regarding my well-being.

I recently told my sister of the event, and she said she never knew that happened. My mother kept it hush-hush and just wanted to shield me from the experience and acted like it never happened. I felt so ashamed, especially since I had to see that boy every day riding the bus to school. I would sit behind the bus driver and press my face against the shield to hide from the boy's gaze, wishing I was invisible. That terrible boy always sat behind me so that he could poke me in the butt with a pencil. I acted like it did not bother me and ignored his taunts. To have a group of children hold you down with a boy on top, mimicking sexual moves, was an embarrassing and humiliating experience. Little did I know that it would become unresolved trauma as an adult. The more I hoped it would disappear from my memory, the stronger the recurrence became. After that experience, my mother was very protective of me my entire life.

I remember the day I got my first period which was the same date as the Pearl Harbor anniversary bombing on December 7th. I was 14 years old. Luckily, I had friends that discussed it. I still did not know what to do or why this was happening. I was fortunate not to get my first menstruation in school. I told my mom, and that's when she bought me pads and briefly explained my menstrual cycle. As time went on, I learned more about my period and sex from my friends in high school. Everyone talked about how sex hurts at first before it gets better, but you can get pregnant. *Well, I hope it doesn't hurt so much,* I thought.

When I finally left The Group over 25 years later, I did a lot of soul-searching. I connected with a sister who left The Group and became a doctor in Atlanta. This sister was giving $10,000 each month to The Group. However, when she visited Daddy Leviathan in Ghana, she was disheartened when she saw babies and toddlers wearing gold chains. She knew her money was not being used to serve any meaningful mission in Africa. She also practiced holistic medicine. She invited me to visit her in Atlanta to help me heal on my road to wellness and wholeness. I did a body cleanse and scheduled a few sessions with an acupuncturist. She recommended that I see Dr. Burke, a local Kinesiologist. Dr. Burke conducted a kinesiology test and showed me how I never resolved that trauma that contributed to my low self-esteem with boys and men. He said that I needed to go back to that time and resolve that issue with those lunchtime bullies. I also had to resolve my issue with my mother. Mom never talked to me about getting my period, sex, dating, or any sensitive matter to help me become a young adult.

Dr. Burke's sessions were helpful, He helped me talk about my past to connect some deeply rooted hurts and pains. Without telling him, Dr. Burke pinpointed the ages between five and twelve were key areas that changed my life-trauma events. First, my father left when I was five years old. Then at seven years old, my life changed drastically when my parents divorced, and I met my stepfather for the first time. A short time after that, I was molested on my elementary school playground.

### Jesus Love The Little Children
*Jesus loves the little children*
*All the children of the world*
*Red & yellow, black & white*
*They are precious in his sight...*

Mom wanted me to have a spiritual grounding. She sent me to Christian Summer Camp in Brant Lake, New York, after the molestation. The location of the camp was in the beautiful Adirondacks of upstate New York, and to this day, I still love the outdoors. The camp's motto was "Holiness Unto the Lord." Every summer from the time I was seven years old to age fifteen, I attended the same Christian camp for one month. Actually, most of my siblings attended this camp at some point in their childhood. The camp was associated with the church that Mom and Dad attended in Woodside, so the camp leaders knew of my family name by the time I got there. My parents were huge proponents of children being trained in the word of God.

For the most part, I enjoyed the camp setting. It was a controlled environment with six girls and one counselor per cabin. We were up by 7 AM and had to make our beds and straighten our room. There were all types of contests, from bed inspection to the neatest girl and other challenges. I tried my best to fold my clothes neatly and make the bed, but I don't recall ever winning. At times, I felt a little out of place because I was the lone Black girl at camp. In fact, during my first year there, I met a five-year-old kid at the lake, and he called me a "nigger." This was the first time I had ever heard the word used at me. Coming from Queens and growing up on Long Island, I did not know what it meant, yet I knew it was bad and belittling. It was a word that was never spoken in our house.

As the years went by, I continued to have my share of macro and microaggressions of racist experiences and white privilege at Christian Summer Camp. Oh yeah, I was also exposed to the Bible, prayer, and being disciplined under strict conditions. But I was also teased about having "fuzzy hair" because I wore cornrows almost every year, which unraveled as the month's stay at camp progressed. There were also times I felt there was a bias against me by the counselors. I felt so unattractive around all of the white girls with long straight blonde and brunette hair. I was complimented only one time in my last year when my hair was permed, and I wore it straight and curly. This did not make me feel good about myself because I loved my natural hair as well. My hair also added to my sense of insecurity as life experiences piled on. Although I had enlightening experiences with the Lord, there were times when I knew my treatment was harsh because of the color of my skin. The camp had high standards of Holiness, but they did not realize they were blinded by white superiority, which has no place in the true Holiness of God.

In my last summer at camp as a 15-year-old, I snapped! I believe everyone has their breaking point, and if someone continues to push your buttons, you will snap. I could not take the snobbish treatment from one of the white girls who, year after year, belittled me and made sure that everyone knew she was extra privileged. I did something I never did prior to or after. I ran and pushed her down to the ground in the middle of her vocal rants against me. Of course, I was chastised very badly by the counselor. Attending a white Christian camp and being verbally abused and mistreated was a precursor to my experience that would begin years later at an Ivy League University in my search for love, joy, and happiness with God. I often asked myself, *How can Christians be so mean?*

During camp worship services, they encouraged us to give our lives to God since we were His children. This act of coming to God was so important to me, and I was excited to do so. I felt God's presence early in my life, and I knew that I was saved. Those early days as a child set the foundation for my outlook on life and how I felt about myself. Although my mom continued to tell me how beautiful I was, I felt ugly on the inside because of my experiences. I had very low self-esteem, yet I was quite athletic as a kid. I loved to run and compete. This was apparent in camp and in my neighborhood. I was always racing kids in the streets when I was home during the summers and through the woods, and during competitions at camp. I was among the best in the athletic competitions—except for swimming.

********

There was always a small spark inside me to achieve and do more, yet it was not directed toward a specific goal. I did not have anyone to sit me down and talk to about what I wanted to do in life. I did not have a parent to talk to me about achieving or striving to do more and be better. Besides James Brown's classic, "Say it Loud, I'm Black, and I'm Proud," I did not have anyone to tell me about loving myself as a Black person. Mr. Brown had no idea how his song impacted me and brought happiness to my heart.

Early on, I wanted to be an astronaut. I also thought of being a doctor, but I knew I could not stand the sight of blood. Then the roles of women began to evolve on TV, and I saw strong independent women like *Charlie's Angels*, *Wonder Woman*, *The Bionic Woman*, *The Mary Tyler Show*, and *That Girl*. I also watched black and white musicals with Lena Horne, and I heard about the history of Madame CJ Walker, an entrepreneur. Then Oprah Winfrey burst onto the scene and stole ratings from Phil Donohue, who was the king of daytime talk shows until she ended his reign.

I am grateful that the positive seeds from the shows were planted inside of me as I secretly wanted to be strong, smart, and courageous like all of the women characters on TV. Oddly enough, I did not see the white heroes as white women but as women role models that I could one day fulfill, despite the racism that I had experienced at such a young age. Sadly, that seed remained deep and tucked away until the appointed time.

## Young Disciples

Dad never re-married after the divorce because mom was still alive, and he believed that if you are divorced, you cannot remarry until your spouse dies. Dad was self-taught in the Scriptures and the ancient Greek language. He was a naturally brilliant genius, always solving the daily crossword puzzles of the *New York Times*. There were times when Timmy and I visited him when my sister was living with him, and I was fascinated as he would encourage me and prophesy over my life. He would take me and Timmy and pray over us with tears sprinkling water over our heads. Dad baptized me in his bathtub as he believed that no one could enter heaven without being water baptized.

The Doctrine of the Apostles is what he named his belief system. He did not have a church building. Instead, his followers would meet with him at his humble abode in Harlem. He did not have a lot of money, but he was the most dignified and classy Black man I had ever seen in my life. He had an incredible vocabulary and spoke with confidence and fire. I knew deep in my heart that he had a connection with God, but I also knew of the bitterness he had in his heart for Mom.

Yet when I met Shirley and Daddy Leviathan, leaders of The Group, on that first night, they will say I got saved for the first time at that moment, which is false. Salvation is a walk with God where we all have a choice to remain with God or go our own way. He will work through people to enlighten us along the way. Those people in The Group were not to be worshiped or held higher than God because only He can communicate to us through whomever or whatever He chooses. Still, that communication should only be a confirmation of what God has already put in your heart.

When my father died, The Group came with me to the funeral. I sang one of the songs from The Group, called "Unity." I put a spin on the song with my own words, and my brother Robert spoke. When my father was in the coffin, he looked so alive, as if he would get up and speak. When we all returned home from the funeral, we talked about how alive he looked in the coffin. We also discussed other folks' testimonials of how he helped people with their lives and gave hungry people food. Daddy Leviathan said, "It looks like I am following your father's example. I'm of the same mold he was made from. Me and your father are kin."

He said this because people were talking about all of the good my father did. In The Group, we were always talking about helping people and providing food. But I would never put Daddy Leviathan and my father in the same light because Daddy Leviathan was a taker—never a giver. Despite my father's sins, he was a giver, and I believe he realized at the end of his life that he was not fair to Mom. Daddy Leviathan continues to stand on his lie that he is free from all sin and is God's gift to us all.

# CHAPTER 4

# Father Figure

*"A good father is one of the most unsung, unpraised, unnoticed, and yet one of the most valuable assets in our society."*
**Billy Graham**

My mother always wanted the best for her children. For two years, we were struggling to make ends meet. Mom was single-handedly raising five children on her own. She took a job working at Macy's and was there for the rest of her working years. She was a member of her older brother's club located in Queens. They went on trips throughout the year to tropical areas. When I look back, I feel so proud that Mom did something for herself after the divorce because she saved up her money and traveled to Bermuda with the club. The man who eventually became my stepfather was the one who picked her up to escort her to the airport for her first trip. He worked for New York City Transit as a mechanic, fixing trains, and was already a member of the club. I'll never forget when she returned all she could talk about was the pink sands of Bermuda! Aruba was the second trip! So Mom secretly married my stepfather, and one day we moved with him to Queens in the dark of night without a moment's notice. My brother, sister, and I got into a big white moving truck with this strange man. His skin was a caramel color, and he wore a happy grin on his face. He was a round, short chubby man—the complete opposite of my tall, lean, and dark brown father.

Most of the time, he smelled of alcohol. I believe this was his closet demon at the time, unbeknownst to Mom. The family packed all of our belongings, and we moved to a strange city and house. My mother never sat me down to inform me that she got remarried and that we were moving. The resentment I had from being uprooted from the only place I knew as a home without any explanation was deeper than I ever realized until Dr. Burke identified that as a life trauma event.

By now, my older brother went into the military, and my next oldest brother was off to St. Paul's College on a basketball scholarship. The years living in Queens with my mom, stepfather, sister, and brother were very difficult. At first, my stepfather bought me an art book which unlocked a gift of drawing that I never knew I had. For that kind gesture, I will always be grateful. However, that was only one of the few things that my stepfather did that brought happiness to my heart.

From the beginning, he made it clear that he was not going to establish a relationship with me as he was steadfast to stay away from even a remote appearance of sexual abuse. Looking back, I realize he must have known someone that was in that situation, and he did not want that to happen to him. Unfortunately, a man's fear, if not managed, will come back another way to get him. He favored my brother over me, yet he was quite distant to both of us in general.

Not too long after we settled into a routine, he began drinking heavily. The booze got so severe, and there were many nights when he cussed us out for breathing. It was terrible, and he got into arguments and physical fights with my sister, who was 15 years old at the time. After a night's upheaval, he would wake up in the morning and act as if nothing happened. The fights with my sister got worse–they were throwing punches, yelling, and screaming. In the meantime, my brother Timmy enrolled in a school and started talking! This was a great time of celebration for us, but it was short-lived because he had to deal with being teased and belittled by students at school because he was in the "special" classes. This was also the time when I was molested at school. I cannot imagine how mom managed all of this and stayed in her right mind. My sister and my Mom also had heated arguments, which also became physical at times. Then one day, my sister was gone. She left to live with our dad in Harlem.

## A Budding Artist

About five years later, my stepfather lost our home in St. Albans, Queens. I came home from school one day and saw all our belongings on the street. My stepfather failed to make his monthly mortgage payments. Myself, Mom, Timmy, and stepdad had to pack up what we could and live with my brother Robert. He had an apartment in Yonkers. If it weren't for Robert, we would have been homeless. I remember we brought our cat, O'Henry, with us, but he got lost walking out of Robert's apartment window. It was quite a stressful time for all of us. But somehow and some way, mom and stepdad secured a home in Long Island, even though it was in one of the most dangerous neighborhoods in the county.

As a 12-year-old, I could even tell the house was cheaply put together. Nevertheless, this was our new home. I never got to say goodbye to any of my neighborhood friends in Queens. I was always an honest gal, and my mom didn't have time to warn me not to say anything to my teachers. So, when I learned how to take the two-hour ride on two buses from Long Island to my junior high school in Queens, I told my friends at school that we moved. Well, the teachers got hold of this information, and I was about to be kicked out since we no longer resided in Queens.

Prior to this, Mom was trying to get me into a private school or Catholic School to keep me protected, but she couldn't afford it. Now that we moved to one of the most dangerous cities in Long Island with low-income families, she had to convince my junior high school to keep me until the end of the school year. Then she pulled off some more magic. Mom spoke to her beautician, who had a shop in Queens, and told of her concerns she had about me going to a rough high school that was predominantly Black and recently had a shooting. This was back in 1978, prior to Columbine, yet the media didn't care about what was happening in low-income Black neighborhood high schools. So, Mom worked out my high school situation. She used her beautician's address, who lived in West Hempstead, New York. Her beautician was married to a white man and lived in a predominantly white community. The plan worked.

# CHAPTER 5

# Following The Crowd

*"Never be limited by other people's limited imaginations."*
**Mae Jemison**

M y high school days were fun. I immediately connected with the small number of Black students at West Hempstead High. Long Island was so different from schools in Queens. Queens was truly a melting pot! I had Black friends, White friends, Phillipino, Dominican—all kinds of nationalities with no obvious dominating race. I was exposed very early to many types of people from different cultures, and it was great. The whites in my high school were not very inviting, but it didn't matter because I had a blast with my friends! We experienced the birth of rap way before it hit the radio. Basement parties filled with so many underground artists with incredible beats. We would talk about this new wave of music at lunchtime and then go to the roller-skating rink. Bounce, Rock, Skate, Roll!

In my neighborhood, there was a big festival with giant speakers that would blow your ears out with the thumping music! Then the rap battles would begin. What is this amazing sound that fascinated us? We had no idea we were experiencing an era that is still highly cherished by my generation, especially all of the boroughs of New York and Long Island. We got it first, then the rest of the world was introduced to the Sugarhill Gang's "Rapper's Delight." Sugarhill paved the way for so many rappers to flourish like Curtis Blow's,

"These Are The Breaks," Run DMC's "Sucker MCs," and so many more. I was always proud of LL Cool Jay because, like me, he is a Queens native.

Looking back, I can see early signs of being more of a follower than the true leader God had ordained me to be. My best friend was excellent at softball and basketball. In my neighborhood in Queens and in camp, all I did was race people. I loved to run. However, my friend encouraged me to try out for softball. I failed miserably at softball. In the 9th grade, I was 5'10 and my best friend was 5'9. Between her and the Junior Varsity Basketball coach's request, I joined the basketball team in the 9th and 10th grades. I was not the greatest, despite my height, so in the last two years of high school I joined the track team where I received many medals and was honored as MVP.

Looking back, I wish I was not so gullible to follow another person's dream. Being a follower ended up being a theme for me for many years to come. It is something that I still need to keep an eye out for. If I started track just two years earlier, I would have peaked earlier in college and who knows what I could have achieved! Nevertheless, I had the time of my life! I remember my teammate playing "Stomp" by the Brothers Johnson while we did our sprint warm-ups to get in the running mood and groove while the lyricist sang "Running, running, running!" Then I couldn't wait for the amazing bass guitar solo and then the keyboard solo that followed.

In high school, I knew I was also gifted in art. I was among the best in my art class. My work was displayed in the annual art show for a couple of years in a row. I loved using pastels, and charcoal! My art teacher encouraged me to apply to the Fashion Institute of Technology (FIT) for fashion illustration. However, I inherently felt that I could not make a career in art, or at least that was my impression at the time. In the tenth through twelfth grades, I did exceptionally well in my non-regents math class to the point I didn't need to study. During my sophomore year, I asked my teacher to be switched to the higher-level regents classes because I was among his top students. Not to mention that I really enjoyed math. This was my first attempt to step up and challenge myself academically.

Being one of a handful of Black students in a predominantly white high school, he told me no, and advised that it was best to stay where I was since I was doing so well. Years later, I realized there was a culturally underlying instinctual motive for keeping me back as a Black girl. My white male math teacher did not see a formidable future for me in math-related fields. When this happened, I had no motive for progressing in life, so I did not put a lot of effort into seeking higher education.

By senior year I went to my guidance counselor because I did not know what to do after I graduated. I told her I liked art, and we discussed the opportunity for me to apply to local art universities. But art did not spark any passion in me. One of my best friends was Jasmine, an extremely intelligent Black girl. Jasmine's parents encouraged learning and higher education which became her goal. She was in the top three in our graduating class. During our senior year, she was such an inspiration to me that I excelled in English and received the English award from one of the strictest senior class teachers.

However, I continued the year with no college plan in sight. After spending time with Jasmine, visiting her beautiful home in Lakeview, and seeing her intelligent and well-spoken parents, the seed was planted in me that I could achieve as well. Her family seemed so stable, with a lack of all the drama and disappointments that I had been through in my short time on earth.

I remember having a heart-to-heart conversation with Jasmine at her home. She said, "You have the personality of dreaming to reach the moon." I'm still like that today, but now I have the Wisdom to guide me.

# PART II
# My Feeding Stage

*The Larva (caterpillar): This is where the caterpillar eats and eats and sheds its skin at least four times. Food is stored and used later as an adult.*

*The beginning of wisdom is this: Get wisdom.*
*Though it cost all you have, get understanding.*
*Proverbs 4:6-7 (NIV)*

# CHAPTER 6

# Teenage Love

*"Some people are made for each other*
*Some people can love one another for life, how 'bout us?*
*Some people can hold it together*
*Last through all kinds of weather, can we?...*
*How 'bout us?*
*How 'bout us, baby?...*
**Champaign**

graduated high school at 17 years old and I had not applied to *any* colleges. I spent my first summer as a high school graduate, running rampant with George, a boy I met at a local shoe store downtown. I was the classic case of going to college because I followed a boy!

George was tall, handsome, and happy-go-lucky. He had light brown eyes and a deep caramel complexion. George was Trinidadian from a well-to-do home on Long Island. We were too much alike: dreamers with no common sense. We believed the world was our oyster; we could go anywhere and achieve anything in life if we wanted to.

George played bass guitar and I watched him play guitar with his friends in the summer of 1982, the year I graduated from West Hempstead High School. I was rogue. We drove all over the place in his four-door silver Honda Civic. We hung out at Jones Beach, concerts, and the mall. I remember we loved Wendy's and ate there often. Although we were carefree that summer, George did something that I had not—he applied to SUNY Farmingdale, now known

as Farmingdale College. At the time, it was a local two-year community college. I had never heard of Farmingdale, but since George was
going, our puppy love was so strong that he encouraged me to apply
so that we could be together forever.

George was studying Electrical Engineering Technology. I applied
for the Biomedical Engineering Technology program which shares
courses with the Electrical Engineering Technology program. This
haphazard, nonchalant decision ended up being the game-changer
that set my life on a positive new course. After the first month in the
program, George dropped out. I continued to excel in my classes.

The more I took my studies seriously, the more George and I
started to argue. I felt the strain of abuse that my mom had when
she argued with my dad and stepdad. One day we were arguing in
Roosevelt Field Mall. To this day I have no idea what the argument
was about. Yet I have the most painful memory of George punching
me so hard in the face that he knocked me out in public. I pressed
charges and took George to court.

Mom did not come to support me in court because she knew I
was in a sexual relationship with George, and I was quite rebellious
that summer. Although Mom never gave me guidance about relationships, I knew in my heart that premarital sex was not right. I
sensed in my spirit that I should not have been running around so
recklessly.

I was sad and hurt because I had to go to court by myself, while
George showed up with his father. I had no support system at home
or elsewhere. Fortunately, I got a restraining order against George.

During the Christmas holiday that year, I told my oldest brother
Brandon what happened. He was shocked and said, "Wow Anna, I
wish you would have told me. I would have shown up to be with
you." My brother's words left a big hole in my heart. I never thought
to ask him to come with me during that time. I was probably too
embarrassed. Although Brandon and I, as the first and last siblings,
never communicated much, to this day I love and appreciate him for
what he said to me. I'm so sorry I never got to tell him that before he
passed away at the young age of 50 many years later.

# CHAPTER 7

# Finding My Stride

*"I didn't want to just know names of things. I remember really wanting to know how it all worked."*
**Elizabeth Blackburn**

Despite my relationship setback, I continued in the biotech area of study. I was a high B student and felt confident in my abilities and comfortable in my secure learning environment. For the second year, I was no longer commuting and I moved on campus. That fall I became Student President of the Biomedical Engineering Society. The members encouraged me to run for Homecoming Queen and I won! I was crowned SUNY Farmingdale's Homecoming Queen.

Homecoming Queen was not just about beauty. We went through a series of panel interviews and had to be students of good standing. My leadership position in the Biomedical Engineering Society was also a plus. The final contestant question was, "Who do you admire and why?" I was going to say my mom, but then the name "Lena Horne" blurted out. "I admire her because not only was she a beautiful singer, and actress, but she was also a civil rights activist who used her talents to help people of color." Bam, just like that I won! I was really blossoming on the outside.

Around that time, Vanessa Williams won the Miss America competition, and it was an amazing boost to all of us Black students, despite the negative attacks that followed her after she won. She has been and will always be an inspiration to me. Yet during that time, deep down, I felt the strain of depression. I felt like something was missing in my life. On the outside, I appeared fine. I was determined to finish my classes on a high note, so I put my head in the books.

I took a non-calculus-based physics class and I discovered my love and talent for math and physics. It was like a light clicked on the inside telling me, *this is what you're supposed to do*. With one Associate's degree under my belt in June 1984, I was hungry for another degree—I didn't want to stop at being a Biomedical Technician. I challenged myself by entering the Farmingdale Engineering school, knowing that the physics classes would be rooted in calculus-based mathematics. The math classes not only included three levels of calculus but also linear algebra and differential equations. The challenge sent a fire through me as I remembered that resounding "no" that my high school math teacher said to me when I wanted to take advanced mathematics. This time I ran straight ahead, full face forward. The mere thought of math made me giddy on the inside.

In the Fall of 1984, I entered the Farmingdale Engineering Science School. I continued to live on campus. I moved there in my 2nd year of studies, and I joined the track team. Without a doubt, the next two years at Farmingdale were the best years of my adolescence. I was running track, which I absolutely loved, and I was studying the most fascinating and great subjects that I was passionate about. I received straight A's in my math classes and averaged an A-minus in physics classes. I befriended a few people on campus and spent most of my free time with the track team.

My friend Chase was a commuter like me in our first year, but he moved onto campus and joined the Farmingdale Rams track team, too. He was such a gentle, kind young man with the greatest smile. He ran the 110 and 400M hurdles. He seemed quite determined in his event but was always banging his foot or his leg on those hurdles. God bless his soul! I always thought he was a bit clumsy. Maybe it was the slight bow-leggedness that made me wonder why he picked that event.

I was dating Chase's friend Clive, who like me, ran the 200M and 400M. Clive and I were like two peas in a pod. Clive was a tall, brown-skinned handsome Jamaican guy and I had no doubts that we would marry and raise a family together. Up to this time in my life, I had never known love as I had with him. All of us on the team had so much fun traveling to track events at other colleges, meeting local athletes, and running at Penn Relays in Philadelphia. There were wonderful memories and bonds made with the track team that has lasted to this day. After I left Farmingdale, Chase, Clive, and many of the people we ran with on and off the track remained in touch...except for me.

Out of the blue, Clive broke up with me a few months before graduation. I was extremely hurt and stunned. Clive was my soul mate, my friend, and my love. Sure, we had arguments, but they were silly and petty. Certainly not enough to break up over. Our last argument led to physical abuse, and I responded in the exact manner my mother did when my father beat her and walked out. Clive literally beat me down to the ground. I got up and begged him not to leave me. I cried hysterically and tried to pull him towards me. He turned his back on me and walked out. I was devastated but determined to finish the studies I started.

I continued to excel in my studies and graduated Phi Theta Kappa with awards in physics and tutoring. I was listed on the back page of Farmingdale's Yearbook under the Profile for Future Leaders: Captain of the Women's Track Team, Homecoming Queen, Phi Theta Kappa, and then accepted to an Ivy League University. By the time I graduated, I received the Physics Award, Tutoring Award for Math and Physics, and the Garnett D. Baltimore Medal for Excellence in Science and Math sponsored by Rensselaer Polytechnic Institute (RPI), a notable Engineering School in upstate New York.

To continue my Bachelor's degree, I got accepted into every college I applied to: RPI, Villanova, Rutgers, and an Ivy League University. My friend Chase went on to study Aviation and Engineering at a local college and Clive continued his four-year Mechanical Technology Engineering degree at Farmingdale when it converted to a four-year college. I was heartbroken over Clive, yet excited to start a new chapter of my life at the prestigious Ivy League University, which was noted as top three in the country for its Electrical Engineering School.

**********

By the age of 21, I was sorely lacking in experiences with positive male role models. I witnessed my father verbally and physically abuse my mother. I witnessed my stepfather verbally and physically abuse my mother and my sister. I was molested by a male peer on the elementary school playground. My first love from high school physically assaulted me. And now, a college graduate with two Associate's degrees, my soulmate physically abused me. The worst part is that I was willing to endure more. I was vulnerable to abuse based on my exposure to it. I remember talking to a male who left The Group, and he said he had been abused in his youth. I questioned myself and wondered why I could not find genuine unconditional love. It took years to realize that I needed to accept and love myself first and true love would present itself to me. Deep down inside I blamed myself for being abused. I gave my abusers a pass and was willing to allow it to continue. I didn't dig deep enough to find out why this pattern was in my life.

From a medical standpoint, psychologists call my experiences Intergenerational Violence. This is when abuse passes through the family, beginning with the older generation such as my parents, and passing down to the children. I think the scary consequence of intergenerational abuse is that the children usually end up in abusive partner relationships based on what they saw in the home. Unfortunately, I fit the mold.

Those who abuse were also probably abused. One evening, I became verbally abusive to a young man that was interested in me during the first two years at Farmingdale. He was a sophisticated, handsome young Black man from a well-to-do family. I secretly had a crush on him a year prior to meeting Clive. I was so happy that he wanted to take me on a date.

Deep down, I felt I was not good enough for him. I told him I entered a talent show and I was modeling in a bikini and asked him to escort me. I had a fantastic, athletic, slim body and got many compliments from everyone that night. Well, the vanity went to my head and when he dropped me home, I burned the bridge telling him he was not good enough for me. This poor young man broke out in tears and for the first and last time, I felt good that I hurt his feelings.

Looking back, this was a psychological game I was playing. I knew of his background and the truth is I felt I was not good enough for him anyway. To this day, I regret hurting him and I wish I could find him to apologize.

There is also secondary trauma experienced by those abused. However, I am living proof that with God, you have the power to break the generational curse of abuse regardless of how long you have been in that negative cycle. The primary step for me was to stop looking for acceptance from others and to love myself unconditionally and sincerely. Ezekiel 18:19-20 says, "If the wicked turn from their way, the curse is broken." It's important that spiritual believers understand they don't have to spend their life working on breaking generational curses. The moment you align yourself with God, He washes away all evils from past generations.

I think about this when I'm watching *The Game of Thrones* and *House of The Dragon* series because they provide a good portrayal of descendants failing because of the sins of their parents as they follow the ways of their ancestors. But I'm so happy that when we turn away from evil, it's important to know that our lives will not remain in these "curses" unless we believe in them and allow them to come back—like becoming an abusive person after being abused for years.

*The one who sins is the one who will die. The child will not share the guilt of the parent, nor will the parent share the guilt of the child. The righteousness of the righteous will be credited to them, and the wickedness of the wicked will be charged against them.*
**Ezekiel 18:20**

Loving myself from within and not through the eyes of others was the first step to freedom. I realized that I could not control anyone else's feelings, but I could choose to love myself by acknowledging and celebrating the beauty and gifts that God has given me. At the same time, I had to acknowledge my shortcomings yet pursue with hope and faith that God will do the refining as long as my heart is willing. This type of mindset is one way that helped me stay positive. No matter what happens, I know for sure that nothing is too hard for God!

*When the righteous cry for help, the Lord hears and delivers them out of all their troubles. The Lord is near to the brokenhearted and saves the crushed in spirit. Many are the afflictions of the righteous, but the Lord delivers him out of them all. He keeps all his bones; not one of them is broken.*
**Psalm 34:17-20 (ESV)**

# CHAPTER 8

# Ivy Leaguer

*"Educating the mind without educating the heart is no
education at all."*
**Aristotle**

My initial Ivy League experience was surreal. In 1986 I arrived on the campus of one of the most prestigious universities in the world. A young woman with no desire to go to college was accepted to an Ivy League University. All I could think about was *If my high school math teacher could see me now*! I was an Ivy League student intending to major in Engineering Physics. I was excited about this new challenge. The campus was beautiful, and my mom came to help set up my room.

Not long before I settled in, I switched from Engineering Physics to Electrical Engineering. I heard a few students saying how hard engineering physics was and how many of their peers did not make it. I switched my major without giving myself a shot. In hindsight, it was another sign of how I could be easily influenced by fear to make me change my life's course.

I recall there was a group on campus that students called, The Genesis Group. This Group was seen as radical, and they had established a negative reputation on campus. Everyone warned me to stay away from The Genesis Group. They told me the story of a girl who was an engineer and she dropped out to follow The Genesis Group. It turns out that The Genesis Group was in fact "The Group." I was surprised to see that this university had tons of religious organizations operating freely throughout the campus.

There were preachers screaming at the top of their lungs in front of the main building by the large clock at High Rise Tower. Hopefully, today there are laws to change on-campus policies to protect students from being exposed to and manipulated by such a myriad of religious beliefs on a college campus. It is mind-boggling how so many cults were allowed to thrive on this campus. There was another popular white male leader, and people would flock around him. His cult was whites only.

If I could take back the moment I met The Group, I would wholeheartedly do so. If I only knew what I was about to walk into and remain for the next 25 years of my life, I would have steered clear of The Group, which already had a presence on campus. Cults thrive on college campuses to influence young adults who are still finding their way in life. I've asked myself the question over and over, *What causes one young adult to fall into a cult's trap and another young adult to see them for who they are and run in another direction?* I don't know about anyone else, but my home life was unstable, and I longed for a father figure. I longed to fit in and be loved unconditionally. At the time, I was still heartbroken from the abrupt break-up with Clive at Farmingdale.

There were many nights when I wished I had a father that could have warned me or sat me down and talked to me about human nature and different personalities. Dad, I wish you would have explained to me about the birds and the bees and protected me from predators. I was so naïve, and I was desperate for a father's love. At the same time, I was in search of seeking a higher purpose. I was seeking God. I heard Him knocking at my heart for many years since I was a child and I turned Him away. As I grew older, the knocking became louder. By the time I entered this new college, I sought an answer to the knocking.

## Keep Running

I had one more year that I was allowed to run on the track team. The clock starts when you graduate from high school, and you are allowed four years plus an additional year if you skipped a year. I was so happy that I could use my final year as an athlete at this Ivy League university. Running track was the only thing I really enjoyed because the university itself was a big culture shock.

The majority of the students were from nuclear, middle-class, or wealthy families. I did not connect with anyone. I felt isolated. I was depressed, lonely, and licking my wounds from the breakup with Clive. I was still in shock over the whole incident, and it left me sad for much of the summer. Thank goodness I kept myself occupied with a job at a local pool and running with a summer track team in Long Island. I admit that I had an amazing summer season and ran my fastest times qualifying for the Empire State Games. I was an underdog in the 200M, and I beat the number one runner who was expected to win the qualifying race. I was on the road to setting goals and being competitive. The weird thing was that I was achieving my goals and it felt great, yet there was still a deep pain in my soul.

In contrast to Farmingdale College, my grades were not the best at this new University. I was struggling because I was still devastated over the breakup with Clive. I also could not connect with the instructors like I was able to at Farmingdale. I was used to 30 students per class. At this university there were hundreds of students per class. As the Thanksgiving holiday approached, I felt like a failure, and I wanted to end my life. There was a spirit of suicide on campus, as there were years and years of incidences where students had taken their lives at the famous suicide Gorge Bridge on campus. I felt that spirit calling me.

I kept thinking about when I went on the tour of this Ivy League University and how the guide actually bragged about this famous bridge where students commit suicide because of the pressure to succeed. They said it so casually. That is such a horrible thing to make light of. I felt like I could not shake the spirit of suicide even though I knew I had a gift in math and engineering.

When I came home the first week before Thanksgiving, I wanted to die. I seriously considered taking all of my stepfather's medication from the medicine cabinet. I could not see a reason to live—I felt like I lost everything. I pushed myself to go back to school after the break and I was glad I did. That's when I met a classmate, a lovely Black girl, named Jenna. Jenna was a petite fireball who loved the Lord. We began to form a bond as I was drawn by her sincere love. She was one of the kindest people I ever met.

I remember going to her apartment to study for the first time. When she answered the door, she brought me in, stepped away, and gave me a cold glass of apple juice. It was the best glass of apple juice I ever had! There was so much love that was transferred from her heart to her hand, to the glass. I believe that was the moment when God slipped right into my heart. No confessions needed. Just a transfer of Divine Love from the One whose cup was full to the one that was thirsty for love.

The next day when I took the bus to campus, I felt lighter and happier. I definitely felt different. For the first time in a while, I felt so much love, and whatever hate or anger I had in my heart for people was dissolved. Jenna and I visited each other and studied frequently. There was a day when we were in my room and I told her I was having issues with my roommate, so she prayed vigilantly with me. As time drew near to my birthday, Jenna decided to introduce me to "the saints" as she called them. This was a common term amongst The Group.

Jenna took me to a large house off campus where about seven students who were part of The Group lived. As I walked in, they were having a prayer service. **Right then I should have turned around and walked out because it was very strange to me at first**. One of the students praying was standing, facing the wall, eyes closed, and talking, and I guess she was "in the spirit." It was the weirdest thing I had ever seen. I put "in the spirit" in quotes because as I got to know that individual later on, she was one of the meanest people I had ever met. Nevertheless, on that day I was walking on a cloud because of Jenna's sincere influence on me. When the prayer ended, the leader of The Group stood up to preach.

Here was a man that had a pimp-like stride with hip-hop-style clothes in his early 30s. I was surprised that the preacher was dressed like a teenager. In the 80s, slicksters wore leather jackets with colorful designs. It was the dawning era of brands like Cross Colors, Fubu, and Black designers that wanted to make a bold statement.

The preacher represented that well in style but was too old to really pull it off. Nevertheless, the style of dress was attractive to college students to bridge the age gap of 10 years that he had on us.

I found the preacher to be unforgivably bold, outspoken, and fiercely confident of every word that came out of his mouth. He had this gift to deliver the word of God with fire, but unfortunately, he was always attacking someone. He called people out and put them on the spot to prove his point. Whether his point was good or bad, he would find someone to fit his desire.

As he spoke, I felt a high degree of conviction from the preaching, and I felt I was being directly attacked. I kept saying, "I'm saved already." He told me to put my hands up and started to prophesy over me. He said, "Something's going to happen with your family." I translated this in my heart that he was speaking in a positive way regarding me being a light to them and making a difference. So, when he said that, I began to weep as my heart was touched.

Then he went in a different direction. His fire and brimstone message caused fear to overtake me as he continued to preach after I refused to raise my hands. I wanted to walk out as fast as I could, so I turned around and headed straight for the door. Right as I got to the door, another leader from The Group, Shirley met me, wrapped her arm around my waist, and hugged me. It was like she felt my pain and let me know without words, she loved and supported me. Right there, I broke down and cried.

All of the stresses of my family life, school, and disappointments were released through my tears. Little did I know that this very moment created a many years-long bond with Shirley. A bond that I wish would have remained as pure as that first hug. In The Group, sincere bonds were impossible because of the idolatry towards the preacher, Daddy Leviathan, who does no wrong in their eyes. A pure bond would have remained true to God's Power of Truth which is greater than any man on earth.

## Perfection

When I first joined The Group, I was writing Daddy Leviathan letters praising him for being a great leader and thanking God for having him in my life. These were the types of things that the members of The Group did, and I was learning about their culture of always praising the Elders because the Elders never sin— they uphold the Scriptures that require us to be perfect. They preached that when you are Born Again, you are made perfect. Perfection was emphasized and preached day in and day out. We all had to be living free from sin. This was the theme of The Group that resonates to this day. First John 3:8-9 (**KJV**) says,

*"He that committeth sin is of the devil; for the devil sinneth from the beginning...Whosoever is born of God doth not commit sin; for his seed remaineth in him: and he cannot sin, because he is born of God..."*

This Scripture was the main one used to keep the congregation under subjection. Accusations of committing sin in the form of having a bad attitude or looking the wrong way were constantly being brought out. The biggest sin of all time was disagreeing with the Elders and being disobedient to them. Daddy Leviathan would often say, "If you're good with me, you're good with God."

The Group came to visit on campus just about every weekend. They would send their top teachers to come and live with some of us who lived off campus. When The Group did not come for the weekend, sometimes I took the bus to New York Port Authority and then took the train from Penn Station to New Jersey. During one of my visits, as I was walking through Penn Station, I noticed a little store that sold yo-yos. I recall Daddy Leviathan playing with a yo-yo a few weeks prior. There was a new light-up yo-yo that I thought would be a perfect gift. I always had a giving heart, and I knew he would enjoy the yo-yo.

Daddy Leviathan loved the yo-yo and played with it all the time. He had the heart of a kid and a great sense of humor, although many times his humor was at the expense of others. Eventually, the yo-yo broke—that's what happens with toys. Right? It was a cheap yo-yo that cost around $2.00. When I returned for another visit, I bought him another yo-yo. He refused to take it because he wanted me to fix the broken yo-yo. I tried but I could not fix it. In the middle of the Bible study, he made me the brunt of his five-minute rant telling everyone that I was studying electrical engineering at an Ivy League University and that I could not fix a yo-yo.

He spoke of how inept I was and how college students have book knowledge but no common sense. He was always quick to knock down education. Yet he made a living off the college students because after we graduated, we were the primary ones who obtained good jobs and supported his lifestyle. Looking back, I see how he strategically went right for the jugular when it came to our pride. Instead of encouraging and celebrating that Black people were in Ivy League colleges, he chose to put us down every chance he got since none of the Elders were educated beyond high school.

I was still new to The Group. Daddy Leviathan's open remarks about me were devastating and caught me by surprise. I was in shock, and I believed this was something I had to take from someone who walked closely with God. I remember when the *Raiders of the Lost Ark* movie came out and I had come home that summer and saw it with some friends. After Bible study, we were talking about movies, and I spoke up about how fun it was and how I enjoyed it. Daddy Leviathan, blurted out, "Yeah, well, that's because you don't have an exciting life. Of course, you're going to like a movie like that because you ain't got nothing else going on in your life!" He had a way of giving eloquent examples to juxtapose your life or situation to something in the Bible and essentially put you down. He always had insulting comments.

Even when The Group formed a band and we were getting our professional group photo done, Daddy Leviathan was standing on the side with some of his other women, and he shouted in my direction, "Look at the ugly one!" For years he said many cruel things to me in front of the congregation. Any time I made a comment, I was deemed disobedient or had a sinful heart. I had to repent and apologize for my actions often and ask everyone to pray for me.

The Scriptures on sin are true. We all have a choice to be obedient to God. But that's the dividing line—obedience to God, not someone who puts themselves in the place of God. It turns out, Daddy Leviathan was and continues to be the biggest sinner of all. Not only was he caught sleeping with married women, but he also fathered children with his nieces and too many young girls to count. So much for living free from sin!

# The Beginnings House of MOTS

## (Ministry of the Shoemakers)

The Bishop (elder)

Ma Shoemaker
(Her children below part of early ministry)

Jerry Shoemaker — Married to Shirley

Anthony Shoemaker

Lela Shoemaker — Married to Daddy Leviathan

Lulu Shoemaker

Sunny Shoemaker

# CHAPTER 9

# Daddy Leviathan: The False Prophet

*Then the LORD said to me, "The prophets are prophesying lies in my name. I have not sent them or appointed them or spoken to them. They are prophesying to you false visions, divinations, idolatries and the delusions of their own minds.*
**Jeremiah 14:14**

In Isaiah 27:1, A Leviathan is a serpent-type sea monster symbolizing Israel's enemies, who will be slain by God. The name Leviathan is also considered a large, powerful whale-like vessel. The Daddy Leviathan who led The Group is all of these things. He used his henchwomen and henchmen to do his dirty work, but in public, he was this larger-than-life vessel of God. He was about 5'10, dark-skinned, with a belly that resembled the late Alfred Hitchcock. Yet when he spoke, his charisma shone bright, and women and men were enamored by his words.

My first impression when I first saw him was that of an imp. He was jumping around giving an illustration of the Scripture that says, "casting down imaginations and every high thing that exalts itself against the knowledge of God." He then segued into how we need to put on the full armor of God so that we can withstand the wiles of the darts of the enemy. The topic that he was preaching on was absolutely fantastic, but the spirit that I got from him was impish. He made people feel guilty and found opportunities to condemn our lives.

As time went on, I started to realize how corrupt he was and that there was no love behind the words that he preached. If there was true, sincere love, in his heart, it would make the word of God more amenable, and people could receive God through Daddy Leviathan's love and not through a fiery message delivered in a charismatic, manipulative way.

Charisma was his strongest gift. He knew how to break down the Scriptures as if he were a biblical historian. He could go back and forth between the Old and New Testaments with ease. During Bible study, he would teach for a while and then have other Elders teach. We were encouraged to participate and raise our hands with questions.

Daddy Leviathan's biggest message was about living free from sin. He often spoke about the choices we make in life and how our response to situations determines our destiny. He preached love and hate, and how we are new creations in God, so we have a new nature and access to all of the wonderful things God has to offer. Everything Daddy Leviathan spoke was very powerful and moving. It was based on Scripture, but at times it was twisted for his personal purpose and gain.

## A Perverted Prophet

To this day, Daddy Leviathan is still the most perverse human being I have ever encountered. One evening we were at a member's apartment for a Bible study and dinner. Everyone was in the living room. I excused myself to go to the bathroom. I passed by a bedroom, and Daddy Leviathan was standing in the bedroom near a mirror with his pants down. He was gyrating his big penis towards me and then swinging it up and down and waving it to emulate the shape of the cross. I stood frozen, looking at this perverted old man; I guess he thought it was funny. His freaky peep show was interrupted when one of the children in the nearby bedroom came running into the hall and said hello to me. He quickly pulled his penis back and zipped up his pants just as the child reached the doorway.

Daddy Leviathan was so obsessed with sex. I have no idea how he found time to read the Scriptures. He used Shirley to exploit us as often as she could. The women he left behind were told to make nude videos to be sent to Daddy Leviathan when he moved to Ghana. Shirley had all of the video equipment set up in a room of the house located in Elizabeth, New Jersey. Shirley would give a quick run-through on using the equipment, and then she walked out and closed the door.

There was another bottom-of-the-barrel sister that was also sexually taken advantage of by Daddy Leviathan and just left behind. Her name was Emily. Emily and I were riding in the car one evening from Bible study. Daddy Leviathan called her from Ghana and he didn't know that she had passed the phone to me so I could hear the most perverse nasty sexual stuff that he said he was going to do to her. He was saying things like, "I'm gonna put my hand up it, flip it, and turn it..." amongst other things that I blotted out of my mind. I had never heard anything so disgusting. This was a perverse man leading a congregation in the name of God. I was so programmed to believe that if he was doing anything wrong, I would go to hell. I really believed this!

There was a time when I needed to see GYNs to evaluate the fibroid illness that continued to grow in my uterus. I had to get an ultrasound in time for evaluation so that my surgery could be scheduled.

Shirley asked me, "Is the GYN doctor female?"

"No. This is a male doctor."

Shirley replied, "Daddy Leviathan made it clear he does not want any of the sisters to have a male GYN doctor."

I was torn because I had to get the test done to meet all of the scheduled dates. Nevertheless, this was a rare occurrence to disobey after I weighed the balances and decided to keep the appointment. It would have taken too long for me to find another doctor. I was very uncomfortable during the ultrasound process, and I felt violated because of the fear tactic that was presented to me. But I was relieved after I walked out of the office. Out of guilt and wanting to at least "tell on myself" before Shirley would, I called Daddy Leviathan in

Ghana to tell him I completed my ultrasound, but I had to go to a male GYN. His response was, "Did it feel good having his hands inside of you?" He continued to say the most disgusting things, but again, I etched his words out of my mind because he made me feel so low and disgusting. I ignored the conversation completely. This was the only way I could rationalize continuing to follow him.

Daddy Leviathan's pedophilia began to show up before he left for Ghana. By now, the ministry was thriving, and professionals were sending thousands of dollars each month to him. He was living in a big black house located in Newark, New Jersey. He had his legal wife and children living on the second floor and seven other "wives" living with him on the third floor. He had his eye on his niece Lucy. Daddy Leviathan began grooming her to be his apprentice. Yes, you read that correctly, his sister-in-law gave him the green light to have sex with her daughter. Lucy was his special disciple. No one could say anything to this 16-year-old girl. Lucy was treated like a princess among us. She went everywhere with Daddy Leviathan.

Rumor has it that a former member of The Group that worked in a medical facility found out that Lucy's mother, Birdie had an abortion. It was said the father was Leviathan. So, it is possible that Leviathan was having sexual relations with a mother and her daughter at the same time. Birdie and Shirley are sisters, and they, along with Leviathan, are in-laws of Lela and Lulu's family. Lucy was one of the nieces of the family unit.

The entire congregation watched as this young girl was chosen to be the successor of the prophet Daddy Leviathan. So, Lucy bypassed all of us older women and men—she out-ranked us as Daddy Leviathan told us that she had a pure heart. I am witness to the fact that Lucy had a great gift. She could preach and was an excellent teacher. Daddy Leviathan let us know point blank that she was spiritually better than us. Yet underneath the cloak of preaching and teaching, he was having sexual relations with his 16-year-old niece. He knew that he could not continue this perverted lifestyle of polygamy and pedophilia in the U.S., so in 1997, he took Lucy and six other women to live with him in Ghana.

He left his legal wife, Lela, and his five children behind in New Jersey. Several years later, he sent for them to come to Ghana. By then, he had more than a dozen wives and countless children. His wife Lela helped raise all of his children that were being born in Ghana, and Shirley started a non-accredited elementary and high school on the property where they lived in Ghana. Ghanaian parents were desperate for their kids to have an education so they would drop their children off and leave them with Daddy Leviathan. They had no idea they were leaving their young girls with a predator. Within no time, multiple girls became pregnant. Shirley also allowed her own daughter to have sex with their uncle Daddy Leviathan. Can you believe that it was an unspoken belief that women would be blessed by Daddy Leviathan's holy private parts?

Daddy Leviathan had the best of both worlds, having sex with mothers and their daughters. Even Lucy's younger sister succumbed to sexual relations with Daddy Leviathan. Does anyone care that Daddy Leviathan's family is vexed with an unclean and abominable spirit? Daddy Leviathan himself taught us a class on the term "Motherf…" which he says comes from an account in the Bible, 1 Corinthians 5 where a man slept with his father's wife. Why couldn't we see also this applied to him at that time? They will all be accountable for their actions and God's judgment.

## A Woman Scorned

Right before I graduated from this Ivy League University, Daddy Leviathan began pursuing me. He started telling me that I was his wife. It made me feel special, since, like everyone else, I had a deep love and respect for him as a leader. For some of us, he was also a father figure. He came across as someone wise and trustworthy. With his powerful messages and the way he taught Scripture, he carried himself with a lot of confidence, like a true warrior of God.

It was funny because he had a gangster-style way of moving and speaking. He was born and raised in Newark, New Jersey, so there was a bit of hardness to him. He wore jeans and sneakers, and a leather jacket, not like your ordinary Baptist or AME Pastor. He always wore the best—top-of-the-line expensive coats, hats, and shirts.

Shirley, his henchwoman and sister-in-law, made sure his clothes were sharp. She ironed, sewed, and did the things for him that a wife would do. I did not think it was weird even though Shirley was married to Daddy Leviathan's brother-in-law, Lela's brother Jerry.

Shirley went out of her way to take care of Daddy Leviathan. Everyone was aware of it, but none of us saw anything sexual about it. Instead, we saw it as a sister taking care of her brother. Yet, when you take a thousand-foot view, it never dawned on me his wife wasn't taking care of her husband. Shirley demoralized his wife, Lela, so Lela kept everything inside while her husband committed adultery under her roof every chance he got.

Since I had a love and respect for Daddy Leviathan, I was on board to have a sexual encounter with him. I knew it was part of an initiation that all of the women went through. I wanted to be a wife. Although I knew he was married to Lela, and I considered her my friend, I assumed she was OK with his lifestyle since many men in the Bible had multiple wives. I really thought I would be highly respected as all the other wives. After Daddy Leviathan and I had sex, the first thing he said to me is that he wanted me to keep it a secret. Soon after, I asked him, "Well, is there going to be a wedding ceremony? When am I going to get a ring?" He said, "No, you are not getting a ring."

I was around 22 years old at the time. I was never one to keep things about my life secret. I never had anything to keep secret. I didn't grow up in a family where people kept secrets or were creeping around. I was always an open and trusting person. So, Daddy Leviathan was teaching me and countless others how to be deceitful.

*This is what the LORD Almighty says: "Do not listen to what the prophets are prophesying to you; they fill you with false hopes. They speak visions from their own minds, not from the mouth of the LORD.* **Jeremiah 23:16 (NIV)**

A short time after that, we were in another sister's car, and Daddy Leviathan was driving me home from Bible Study. When he pulled up to where I lived, I confronted him and said, "You don't love me!" He looked in my direction and began to cry. It was the most bizarre thing because I expected fire and brimstone. Nevertheless, I left the car because I was hurting. Now I had to carry the burden of keeping my sexual encounter with the prophet of God during a time when Daddy Leviathan's infidelity was not an open fact throughout the congregation. This was the one and only time Daddy Leviathan showed empathy toward me. After that day, he hardened his heart towards me and was cruel to me from that point forward.

There were several other women whom he was more intimate with, and they were all living with him in Elizabeth, Irvington, and then the Black House in Newark, New Jersey. Daddy Leviathan's other women and "wives" were finally revealed to us in the congregation after he moved to Ghana, Africa, where polygamy is legal. It was not long before many young girls and young women were popping up with babies impregnated by Daddy Leviathan. There were two sets of women: those who were part of his harem and those who were like me, not part of the Elite, but we had sex with him as an act of control. Women like me were not allowed to live and travel with him. Many were like me who, after a few encounters, were never touched again.

There were about nine females, which did not include his wife Lela. The Elders and Daddy Leviathan's nine women all traveled in a van together prior to moving to Ghana. There were twins Mia and Maya, recruited from Montclair College in New Jersey, Shirley and Shirley's sister Birdie, her daughter, and Daddy Leviathan's niece Lucy and two sisters from Long Island. No one else was allowed to be in that van. So those of us that were not traveling around with him or not his regular side pieces didn't know about each other until years later. We all knew the unspoken truth that *he took all of his Elite women to Ghana and left us behind.*

As the years went on and there were a few times in a row that I visited Daddy Leviathan in Ghana, where he lived with his multiple wives openly. By this time, he was having babies with underage girls. I had sent word that I needed to talk to him because I was confused about my "spiritual wife" situation with him, and I wanted clarity on my role and status. He had a double personality. He would openly tell you off and dare you to challenge him. He'd shout at you in public and dare you to say things back. Yet when it came to one-on-one conversations, he was a coward. He completely avoided me. He used Shirley and other henchwomen to do his speaking.

I flew nearly 3000 miles using the only vacation time I had after working hard and sending money to support him and his wives in Ghana. Daddy Leviathan would not give me the time of day. I had the same question for him after at least 18 years of celibacy and dedication to him, "What is this type of relationship? Am I one of your wives?" Since I had been asking this question and getting no answer from him, one night in Bible study, Shirley openly stated, "Daddy Leviathan has many wives as well as his 'spiritual wives' who he will never touch again, but they belong to him." Shirley's response was supposed to be my answer.

To me, that was the most torturous state of being that could ever be imposed upon a woman. A man tells you that you are his wife, yet he doesn't want you anymore and will never touch you again. However, you cannot be with another man because you belong to him. *What in the world is this?* I internalized this crazy situation throughout my years in The Group. My internal pain manifested into sickness.

After over 18 years of waiting to be a wife, I was afraid that if I didn't prove my faithfulness to Daddy Leviathan, I would be cast aside. Although there were other brothers in the congregation that I did have my eyes on, they were creeping just like him. The Group was a secret sex pool of men with different females, and one of them, a married guy named Jim, tried to pursue me. I found out later that Jim's wife was with Daddy Leviathan. The ridiculous thing about the environment was that even though Jim knew that Daddy Leviathan and his wife were together, he was content and on the prowl. It was like a little game the men were playing with women.

Jim ended up leaving his wife and kids and moving to Ghana with Daddy Leviathan and his crew. The story gets stranger because Jim was also pursuing Shirley's daughter, Ginny, who also had sexual relations with Daddy Leviathan. Maybe Jim aspired to have a harem of women like Daddy Leviathan since polygamy was allowed in Ghana. What kind of men are these? Jim missed the beautiful years of raising his daughters. He failed to be there for them as a father during the most important times of their lives. There was so much infidelity between spouses and third parties stemming from Daddy Leviathan's perverse nature. Daddy Leviathan's fornication and adultery were out in the open and even celebrated with the arrival of new babies when he moved to Ghana.

Waiting all these years for a ring and validation from Daddy Leviathan, I felt like I was cursed. I had become a nun, not by choice. I wanted to have my own husband and children someday. I was confused, and I kept asking myself, *why can't I be honored as his wife? And if it's legal in Ghana, why can't he have legal ceremonies of marriage to honor not only me but all of the women that are with him having his babies?* This standstill crushed every dream that I had about my future. It was devastating. The last thing I wanted to believe was that he just used me. Of course, that was a fact, and I just wasn't ready to accept that because I believed that men of God do not act that way.

My internal turmoil told me that I was used by Daddy Leviathan. I felt so unclean and dirty on so many levels. The irony is that throughout Daddy Leviathan's teachings, I was convinced that multiple wives were of God. He taught a great deal from the Old Testament, which is full of polygamy. King David was highly favored by God and had multiple wives. Then he preached on nature analogies like the lion and multiple lionesses, justifying that creeping around was OK and of God. He would boast, "Look for yourself, it's right there in the Bible where plenty of men have multiple wives."

Every few months the congregation in New Jersey was sending money to Ghana to celebrate the birth of another one of Daddy Leviathan's children. He went through a lot of young girls and had kids with them. Living a lavish lifestyle with funds pouring in from the U.S., there was no reason for Daddy Leviathan to ever return to New Jersey.

## Lust, Hedonism, and Lies

What was preached in The Group was close to the pure word of God in the King James Bible most of the time. The word would be spoken, taught, and preached every night for half the years I was there. Then in the U.S., it set back to Monday, Wednesday, Friday, and

Sunday in the new millennium after "Daddy" moved to Ghana with his "wives." Despite the fact that the gospel of Love was preached fervently, especially in the early days, behind closed doors, members of the congregation were being taken advantage of. Leviathan found a slick way to pervert the gospel and put distance between us and the true savior Jesus Christ. Instead, he said "Jesus was a fisherman, and "Vuai" means fisherman in the Ghanaian language." This set us on course to pray and call upon the name of "Vuai" instead of Jesus or Jeshua, His true name. After I left The Group, through prayer I was enlightened and immediately stopped using this name that they still call upon to this day. To me, this was abominable to lead people to call on God by a name that is not His.

# CHAPTER 10

# Grooming

*"It is important to remember that, for the most part, people don't join cults. Cults recruit people."*
**Dr. Steven Hassan**

Looking back, I realize that the night I first met Daddy Leviathan I did not feel love from him. Instead, I felt threatened and fearful. I was always second-guessing my words and actions for fear of being ridiculed or ostracized. I was fortunate to form a bond with a Bishop from upstate New York who was a former Elder of The Group. As the years went on and I got close enough to tell him of my desire to leave The Group, he prayed for me and encouraged me to follow God's direction. During our conversations, he told me that the fear tactic is what cults use to ensnare their victims. His advice and guidance are what ultimately gave me the courage to leave. Below is a letter that The Bishop wrote to me a few weeks after I left The Group.

My dear daughter and friend,

Shalom! May the peace, tranquillity, and blessings of Jehovah be your daily blessings; and may he be your guiding principles. The step you have taken will not be without question on your part but remember your trust is not in feelings alone but in faith. As I have told you ⬛⬛⬛⬛ used the fear tactic; but greater is the Holy Spirit within you than any force of evil or darkness. I am praying that your faith fail you not but becomes stronger daily. Keep in the WORD and seek G-d for understanding. I pray that you will be able to find G-dly brothers and sisters you can fellowship with.

I kept looking for you letter and was overwhelmed with joy when I finally heard from you. I trust I have won your confidence and trust. You will never know how happy I am that you have been set free. With me let us pray for others to be set free and move on in G-d. I am always here if you have questions or need special prayer. I will be arriving on Thursday afternoon, Dec. 27 and leaving Tuesday, Jan. 2. Trusting to seed you. I'll be at ⬛⬛⬛⬛. But you have my cell phone number. Keep the faith, hold fast to your deliverance.

Peace and Love, Bishop

*Bishop*

Bishop ⬛⬛⬛⬛ INC.
International Prelate
⬛⬛⬛ Avenue
Buffalo, NY 14203
Email: ⬛⬛⬛
Phone: [716] ⬛⬛⬛
Mobile: [716] ⬛⬛⬛

Daddy Leviathan was the exalted "Pastor," "Prophet," and "Elder" that everyone respected and feared. He supposedly spoke words directly from Heaven. The Group constantly reminded us that prophets are never to be questioned or challenged. If you do so, you are making yourself an enemy of God against His anointed one. In the early days, each time I attended a Bible study there were more and more students and other adults attending. The Group's influence was growing rapidly.

The Elders of The Group had what I call a "sin-meter." They assessed everyone's actions according to sin, yet they could do no wrong. The Elders constantly chastised us by saying, "If you choose to sin, then you are not with God anymore." Deep down inside, I wanted to go to Heaven, but I felt that I had a rotten heart. I wanted a relationship with God, yet I kept doing things wrong—at least according to the Elders.

The Elders were not accountable to anyone, but the congregation was accountable to the Elders. There were days when I thought to myself, *What If Daddy Leviathan is right*? I imagined that if he was living clean with all of the teaching and students behind him, he would have had the biggest impact on the planet. I was willing to do anything that I could to make an impact on the Earth and make it to Heaven.

Jenna, my friend at this Ivy League University, and I used to read 2 Peter 1 which tells us that when you take on the spirit of God you have His character and you can live a good, clean life. We both wanted this prayer to manifest in our lives. The next year, Jenna left for another college, and I lost touch with her. I know she had no idea what was really going on in The Group with the "saints" that she introduced me to.

The "saints" were grooming students like true predators. During my first year, Daddy Leviathan and all of his women were appointed as the top teachers and leaders. One weekend they all came to my apartment off campus. The evening felt harmless and we talked and shared about God and other things going on in the world. When they left, I felt the worst betrayal that I had felt in my life. They read my private journal that I never shared with anyone. I was devastated and embarrassed.

In my journal, I had written that my goal was to make it to the Olympics regardless of how many years it would take. I had committed to a workout and eating schedule and I was really excited about it. It was a deeply personal thing I desired, even if it was a long shot. Someone broke into my private journal and wrote on the top page of one of my workouts: "You need to seek God above all things!" I took it as a reprimand, and I was crushed. I could not believe that they looked through my personal belongings. I didn't even notice that they slipped away from everyone else in the room. I don't know why those words were so hurtful to my soul, but I allowed them to seep in.

In retrospect, although they portrayed themselves as ones who move in the spirit of God, and above "common believers," they had warped pre-disposed pictures of what a ministry was. How dare that person assume going to the Olympics was not a God-given aspiration! Nevertheless, it really got to me and my performance on the track spiraled downward. In 1988 Flo-Jo broke world records in the 100m and 200m which still stand to this day. Her achievements left a resounding impact on me and I believed I could be a superhero and look good doing it as she did. And now, especially with this newfound faith in God, I was believing to the highest about my future and my dreams of going to the Olympics. After all, the Elders always taught "All things are possible with God."

The next month The Group visited again to watch me in a track meet. They said they were coming to encourage me. It was the worst race I had ever run in my life. I lost my confidence. It was like their tactics were working. For years to come, my Olympic dream was the joke of The Group. They openly mocked me. That was another tactic. Once they found something precious to you, they used it to deplete you. I was on the cusp of finding happiness and peace within myself and the Elders did everything they could to cut away chunks of who I was, to the point that as the years progressed, I did not know who I was anymore. I was belittled, chastised, and mocked on a regular basis. The Elders' treatment of me became a trail of self-hatred. I was convinced I was never good enough.

I desperately wanted to be exalted in The Group, to grow in Christ, and be among those trained to deliver the gospel. My vision of being exalted was vain because I associated popularity and exaltation as a result of having great favor with God. But the truth was really about Daddy Leviathan's favoritism, not God's. Why create a culture to compete for God's favoritism anyway? Besides, they always said we were in the 'School of the Prophets" and I believed it with great excitement!

## A Close Watch

The key to keeping the saints under the control of the Elders was to keep a watchful eye on our every move. We were required to be at Bible Study six days a week. During my second year four of us rented another house and I moved in with all of the "saintly" students. The teachers and Elders came by every weekend and we cooked together, sang together, and did Bible study. There was always one saint going back and reporting to the Elders about *any* and *everything* that we did. I didn't realize this was a practice until I moved in with The Group in New Jersey after I graduated.

They sent different teachers to stay with us at our off-campus home on Aurora Street in Ithaca. Some teachers were kind and others were mean. After a while, I did not know how to anticipate the visits, which teacher was coming, and will they be fun or will they be demeaning and full of "look in the mirror judgment" conversations. The joy of being saved had diminished before I graduated in 1989.

After my one year on the track team, my last two years were spent on my school studies and Bible Study-filled weekends when the "saints" came. Aside from forming bonding relationships with other students in The Group, I no longer knew how to have real fun anymore. I wanted to quit school many times, yet I am grateful that Shirley convinced me to finish and get my degree. I know it was only God's grace that I graduated.

As the years went on, there were fewer and fewer people coming to the Bible studies. By the time I graduated, there was only *one* other person still there. I was in too deep and could not see a way out. The Group was all I had. After graduation, I moved into a house with Daddy Leviathan, his wife Lela, and their five children in Elizabeth, New Jersey.

## Guadeloupe

It was the desire of everybody in The Group to go to Guadalupe because they were beginning to establish a following there. Every few months there was a certain number of people from the Elite team selected to go there with Leviathan. Then some of the non-Elite people were selected to go. If you were selected it was the greatest moment. My friend Darla made her famous mark during a Bible Study preaching to the high hills "I want to go to Guadaloupe!" She expressed the heart and soul of us non-Elites. When I graduated I was scheduled to go in the summer of 1989.

When I moved to Elizabeth, I asked Shirley about who is handling the plane tickets. She said, "Oh you are paying for your own ticket." I was good with that. But the interesting thing was that I believe I experienced my first robbery from her. Mom threw a big graduation party for me at home and I collected $865. That was a lot of money back then. Being that I am an honest person, I told Shirley and she took all of the money, telling me it was going towards my plane ticket. I know for sure now, she paid for the ticket and used the rest on Leviathan and his women.

Going to Guadeloupe was a much-anticipated place where boots are on the ground and you experience the ministry in action with the Guadeloupean locals. The anticipation was all around being able to help these people, encourage them and teach the word of God. Also watching the Elite teachers in action was also part of the experience. We all believed that going to this place would evoke a spiritual Holy Spirit baptism where our gifts of teaching, preaching, and exhortation would ripen and surge. It was the experience everyone wanted to have.

Unfortunately, when I got there, from the jump, something just did not feel right. I and another non-Elite sister became the brunt of all the lowest things that could have ever happened. We did have some good Bible study classes that came out of the Bible but then many of the nights were games to attack and belittle people. We would sit around and vote on who has the best hair, who has the ugliest feet, who has the worst attitude, who can preach the best, who is the ugliest in the room, and the list goes on. Since I was always the brunt to the point where on the last night of the trip, I openly told everyone, "You can say what you want about me. I know y'all don't like me."

What was interesting about that trip was there was a local family that loved me. They asked me to spend the day with them and prepared a meal for me. They had not invited anyone else. So, I had one day of relief away from The Group. All of us were living together in one single house and it was dreadful. I, along with the other non-Elite suffered three weeks of constantly being put down by the Elite and Daddy Leviathan. It was the worst experience that I ever had in my entire life at that point. I was being laughed at and mocked, but I could never respond. Even if I wanted to say something during Bible study to expound on the Scriptures, people would suck their teeth. I just had absolutely no respect. They claimed this was boot camp ministry and the non-Elites needed to be treated like soldiers. The tests were supposed to provide character-building and promote us to see how we can be better. But this was more like character assassination.

Living with the Elites in Guadeloupe for a month and not having a friend, or having anybody on my side was my first experience of great loneliness and rejection. This would set off years of me having the same experiences in different settings. During that trip I couldn't wait to get on the plane and never go back because the treatment was not out of love, but from hate. It was done to break me down. When I look at the pictures of how I looked back then, I was a beautiful young woman. But I didn't have the charisma needed to win people over. We were all renting a house on the second floor and I saw Daddy Leviathan go into a private room below with one of his women. He was getting his freak on the whole time.

Before we left, unbeknownst to the rest of The Group members, the Guadeloupians found out that Daddy Leviathan was having sex with one of their local females that attended the Bible studies. That was our last trip. They kicked him out and told him to never come back. So that's how the "godly" Guadalupe Ministry ended. I remember returning from that trip and one day I was standing at the door of the house in Elizabeth, New Jersey. I looked outside and I wanted to leave. But I had nowhere to go and I didn't have a job. When I graduated from college and moved to New Jersey, I broke ties with my family because I was already programmed to believe that if you go back home to your mother then you're nothing. The message from The Group was that you haven't accomplished anything, and you failed because you didn't take in the truth about yourself. Shirley would always quote Ma Shoemaker, who said, "If you can't take it, you won't make it." So if I couldn't take being reprimanded, insulted, and disrespected, then I'm not going to make it to Heaven. More than anything, I wanted to make it to Heaven so that's why I stuck it out.

## Backstabbing and Backbiting

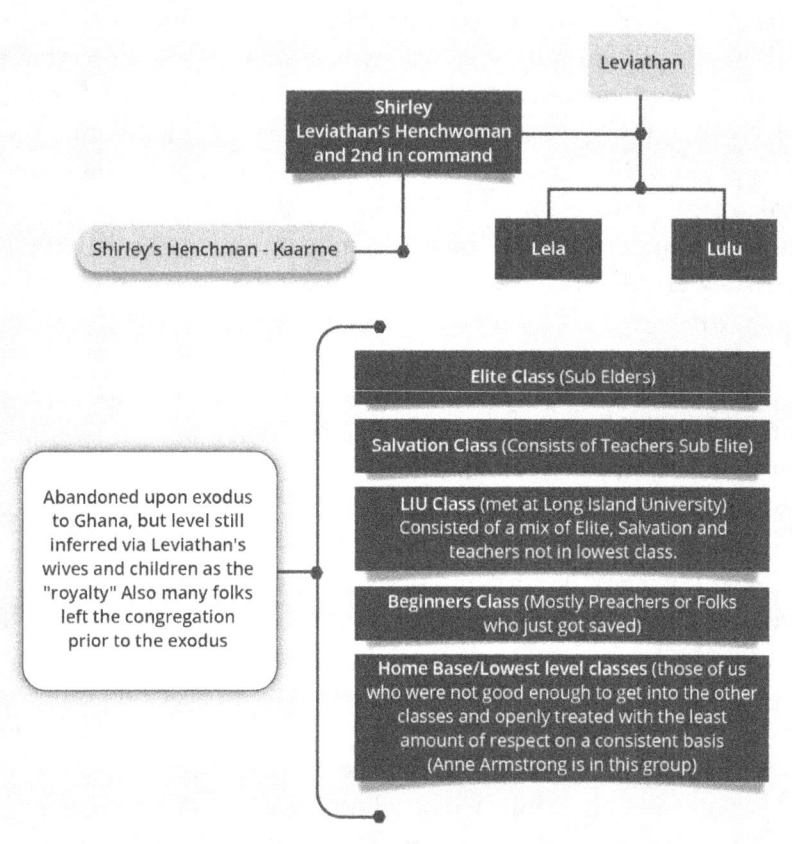

### THE GROUP CULT FORMATION

The early caste system of The Group after departure from Ma Shoemaker

Leviathan

Shirley
Leviathan's Henchwoman
and 2nd in command

Shirley's Henchman - Kaarme

Lela

Lulu

Elite Class (Sub Elders)

Salvation Class (Consists of Teachers Sub Elite)

LIU Class (met at Long Island University)
Consisted of a mix of Elite, Salvation and
teachers not in lowest class.

Beginners Class (Mostly Preachers or Folks
who just got saved)

Home Base/Lowest level classes (those of us
who were not good enough to get into the other
classes and openly treated with the least
amount of respect on a consistent basis
(Anne Armstrong is in this group)

Abandoned upon exodus
to Ghana, but level still
inferred via Leviathan's
wives and children as the
"royalty" Also many folks
left the congregation
prior to the exodus

The true culture of The Group was one of constant belittlement, backstabbing, and backbiting. So many times I was in shock when someone reported me to the Elders. Somehow I always found myself in trouble for speaking my mind or for asking questions about things that honestly did not make sense. I was always shot down, cut off, and ridiculed. "Shut up Anna," rang out of the mouth of the Elders and the Elite often. The Elders and Leviathan created a caste system starting with themselves: Leviathan, Shirley, Lela, and Lulu, then the Elite class, then the Salvation class, and then further sub-classes. This let people know just where they supposedly stood spiritually. I was in the lowest level classes and we were belittled and reminded of our place often by the Salvation and Elite class members. The atmosphere was so childlike and the Elders were always pitting us against each other. Just like in Guadeloupe, there were always discussions and games about who had the best attitude, who had pretty feet, who had ugly feet, who had the best hair, who had the worst attitude, and so many more negative childish things.

If you were on the ugly list, then basically everyone could hurl insults at you and treat you like garbage. I admit, sometimes it was comical when I wasn't the butt of every joke, but it often got heated because people took it too far. I hated that the Elite team could say anything they wanted to you and the Elders backed them up. It was a culture of the haves and the have-nots depending on which team you were on. I was told by one of the brothers that all of the brothers had secretly voted me as the most beautiful of all of the sisters, but they would never publicly say it because Daddy Leviathan's women were pranced around and showcased like they were the fairest beauties of all. I was treated badly, but Emily had it even worse than me. So much about The Group was cruel, ungodly, and hateful.

My biggest struggle was that I always wanted to be in good graces so that I could be guaranteed the praise of being right with God. Basically, if you're "right" with Daddy Leviathan, then you're right with God. Any disagreement with Daddy Leviathan about his lifestyle meant that your soul was in danger. Everyone in The Group believed this because it was what he preached day in and day out and year after year. The problem was that he regularly demonstrated sins in the dark, unbeknownst to us at the time. He impregnated a married woman. He slept with underage girls and impregnated them.

Prior to approaching me, I had no idea he was a predator and was having his sexual thrills with the sisters on the Elite Team. In secret, he smoked a lot of weed and drank a lot of Budweiser with his concubines. He was angry. He yelled. He chastised everyone and accused us often of not being spiritual enough. He was pure evil. Oftentimes, he would have a major tantrum and threaten to leave us, and then on cue, Shirley would appear and beg him to stay and bow down. It was a real show-stopping performance.

The Shirley performance is still so vivid. She would stand in front of him, hold her hands out and say, "Let me stand in the gap for the people, please don't leave, please Daddy, Father don't leave us!" Now, in reality, where on God's green earth was he going? We were financially supporting him and all of his wives and children one hundred percent. Daddy Leviathan had a real stronghold over the female congregation through his sexuality and his perverseness. He also had a stronghold over the men until they found out what he was doing. As the years passed, most of the men dropped out of The Group.

# CHAPTER 11

# True Love Blockers

*"The course of true love never did run smooth."*
**William Shakespeare**

I n thinking back to my days at the Ivy League University, I met
Amaro, a student who had been attending The Group Bible study
before I got there. Seeing Amaro for the first time is so vivid, like
the fresh spring air after a sun shower. He was one of the most
handsome young men on campus! He was tall, dark, and strong
with chiseled features and was a member of the University football
team. His voice was deep, yet with all of the strength he had, there
was a kindness that attracted me to the core of my being. I don't
know if anyone else ever saw his kindness because as the years
went on, he developed a hard callous to protect himself from the
harsh environment that The Group created.

I officially met Amaro around the time I got saved in The Group.
We saw each other on campus often up to the time he graduated,
which was a year before me. One day I was in the library, and as he
passed by, he looked at me and noticed a difference. He said, "You
got saved!" with a big smile on his face. He saw the happiness that
was not there previously, and I was surprised by how perceptive he
was. I always thought he was handsome, yet he also perfected his
gift of teaching. I never told him that I had a crush on him. When
he graduated, Amaro lived in the brothers' house in Elizabeth, New

Jersey. When I graduated, I lived in Daddy Leviathan's and Shirley's houses in the same town where they shared a connected two-family home on Walnut Street.

When Daddy Leviathan originally approached me about being his "wife," I told him my heart was with Amaro.

"Wait a minute, I don't want to be with you, I want to be with him," I said to Daddy Leviathan. He looked at me and told me firmly that I was his and deep down inside, my heart dropped in disappointment. Then about two or three years down the road, there was an evening when Daddy Leviathan and the Elite Team put on a romance play. They performed a song, and he preached about the cycle of the moon and its romantic effect on the ocean's kiss on the rocks under the beauty of a starry night. The room was decorated beautifully as an artist in The Group painted canvas scenes on the walls of glittery rocks and other props. Neither myself nor Amaro knew we were going to be set up. A few weeks before that, Daddy Leviathan told me that I would be tested soon. I was such an airhead! I had no idea what he was talking about and paid it no mind at the time.

The room was dark, so it made the atmosphere even more dramatic. After the characters went through their lines and songs, Daddy Leviathan called Amaro and me up to the front of the room. He told Amaro to get down on one knee and to repeat after him, "Anna, will you marry me?"

Everyone, including me, was shocked! Amaro willingly got down on his knees and willingly repeated Daddy Leviathan's words. I said, "No" and began to cry. I felt that I had to be faithful to my husband, Daddy Leviathan. That's what I was programmed to say and feel because the day he told me I was his, although I still desired Amaro but knew I could never be with him. Yet two years had gone by and Daddy Leviathan had long since kicked me to the curb. So at this point, I was severely confused. Daddy Leviathan called me to the side to talk. I was still weeping feverishly, and He said, "You see, this is how I want you to be. This is how I like you!"

"How am I going to marry him if I'm supposed to be your wife?"

"That's alright. You can be with him, but I just want the firstborn."

This set me on an emotional roller coaster. If I was not mentally ill before, then I was mentally ill at that point. Daddy Leviathan made it clear he wanted to father my first child while being married to Amaro. To this day, it is still hard for me to explain how I tried to process these events.

Even though I told Amaro no, shortly after the Romance Night, I let him know that marrying him was something I wanted to do. I started to build a friendship with him and from that point on, there was this rivalry between Amaro and Daddy Leviathan. I guess I was failing the test because I was secretly happy that God had answered my prayers concerning Amaro. Yet I knew I would not cheat on Amaro with Daddy Leviathan because Amaro was the one I really wanted to be with from the beginning.

Then evil Kaarme came between us. Kaarme is one of the sub-Elites. In retrospect, a few of the brothers both inside The Group and some that left told me that Kaarme had made passes at them, fondled them in their sleep, and had strongholds over them. He was King of the Brother's house and Shirley's henchman, so he was above chastisement. Kaarme knew all of the inside secrets of the Elders and they knew his, so they let him do and say whatever he wanted without reproach. I know Kaarme told Amaro that I was one of Daddy Leviathan's women and was in Amaro's ear, telling him negative things about me, not because he cared about Amaro, but because he wanted Amaro for himself.

So, the day finally came when Amaro asked me if I was one of Daddy Leviathan's wives. I answered, "Yes, but I love you, and I want to be with you!" He was crushed.

"I don't want used goods," was his response.

Amaro's words stung deeply. It was one of the lowest moments in my life. His words sounded just like Kaarme's words. *What was I supposed to do? The man that I was falling for called me used goods.* Then things took a deeper dive when Amaro started playing psychological games with me. He would come back a day or two later and say he still wanted to marry me. Amaro presented me with beautiful ideas for our wedding day. It was going to be a Leap Year, and he wanted to get married on February 29th on top of The World Trade Center. His ideas were romantic, and I was ecstatic.

He was becoming disgruntled with the Elders as their cover was blown concerning me and rumors of other sisters being with Daddy Leviathan. He talked about each Elder that he hated. I didn't know he was beginning to see them for the evil false prophets that they were. Amaro became very angry and bitter with The Group. Now I became a pawn between Amaro and Daddy Leviathan. Amaro knew what Daddy Leviathan was doing with all of the other women, and he hated him. Amaro was hurt because he really looked up to Daddy Leviathan. Very quickly, I watched Amaro turn into a really mean person.

Nevertheless, we were still going to be together, despite all of the drama. Then I spoke with the Elders to tell them that we had a wedding date of February 29th. They told me that I should wait. When I told Amaro what the Elders said, I will never forget the look on his face. He stepped back, and it was as though I threw a javelin right into his heart. It crushed him. I didn't think it was a big deal because I was willing to wait for him, but in retrospect, I now understand that he saw what they were doing.

After that, Amaro made plans to leave The Group and turned his back on me. Before he left, he had sex with one of my dear friends in The Group. I was hurt even more, but knew in my heart he did it to hurt me. Then Amaro left and married a girl from his home state.

At the time, the Elders tried to soften the blow by telling me he never loved me and I believed them. Amaro went on to have two beautiful children but then divorced after a few years. Amaro's departure sent me into a deeper state of mental illness and physical illness began in the form of uterine fibroids. Everything went downhill for me. I guess I failed the test because I had to deal with the consequences of choosing Amaro over Daddy Leviathan and plans of infidelity did not go the way Daddy Leviathan had set up. Years later, I connected with Amaro once and he told me that he really did love me and this gave me closure.

Daddy Leviathan's mind games continued. One day he said to me, 'Why don't you go and just follow Amaro? You are a bad example to the others!" I was flabbergasted and confused. *How could this man, my spiritual husband, say I'm a bad example and he is riding around in a van having orgies with women every day?* This was so crazy.

After the Amaro incident, Kaarme started calling me out, saying I was crazy and stupid, and other negative comments. Everyone laughed at me often and I became the butt of jokes. Amaro saw all of The Group's tactics coming so he left. *Why didn't I leave with him?*

# CHAPTER 12

# Music For The Soul

*"Awwww Feeeveerrr! Burning Hot!! Burning in your flesh"*
**Lyrics From The Group's Song, Burnin**

Early on, after I graduated I moved to New Jersey to live with The Group. I actively participated in the plays and musical performances at high schools, elementary schools, churches, and eventually at clubs. We also composed original music that was cultural, and uplifting people of color. We grew out our perms and wore our hair natural. One good thing that came out of my experience is that I haven't permed my hair since college and I learned to love my natural hair.

The music we created and played was very good and inspiring. Our music was earthy and funky and we were often compared to the hit group Arrested Development. Daddy Leviathan did not want our music to sound like church music and in fact, he did not call himself a Christian because he said Christians were bad examples. He would say out loud, "I hate Christians!" And we all followed suit.

We had singers, dancers, and talented musicians playing horns, flute, bass, and guitar. The band was all female with the exception of Daddy Leviathan on the drums. I was a background singer and they made sure to keep me in the back while he showcased his young 16-year-old niece and Padawan, Lucy. At the time, we did not know he was having sexual relations with her, as well. By the time I left The Group, Daddy Leviathan's niece had two children with him.

During all of this, we would sing a song called "Burnin'" to encourage the congregation and anyone else who heard us sing, to abstain from sexual relations because our body was a temple that belonged to God. Here is a sample of a few lines of the lyrics of this song which were very strong and felt like the singers were in a conversation:

> *Singer #1: God knows my heart, He will meet my needs*
> *Singer #2: You're still burning cause you're yearning with desire,*
> *you're on fire cause you can't contain, abstain, refrain yourself*
> *The solution, complete absolution is to wait,*
> *take your time, don't give in*
> *Give your heart, you're mind, your body your soul He'll take control*
> *A lesson on sanctification, illumination, and consecration*
> *Get real, your heart ain't right!*

Looking back, I can understand why there was such turmoil in my soul, knowing that Leviathan was causing us to be in whoredom with him as we sang this song at the top of our voices hundreds of times. All along he was having sex with his extended family members and females in The Group's band.

Lucy's mother, Birdie, and Shirley were sisters. Shirley and Daddy Leviathan married into the Shoemaker family: Daddy Leviathan married one of the twins, Lela, and Shirley was married to their brother, Jerry. We sang uplifting love songs that could be interpreted as love between a man and woman or with man and God. We sang about good hair, bad hair, and being proud to be Black in a funky, R&B manner. The Bishop told me that the only good thing The Group had going for them was the music. I tried to write songs with The Group but they got rejected because they claimed my songs did not go along with the sound they wanted to create. I thank God that after I left The Group, I picked up songwriting again.

There were a few highlight moments singing with The Group when we performed at popular New York City comedy and jazz clubs including *Carolines* and *Sweetwaters*. I met up-and-coming celebrities like Chris Tucker and Mike Epps. This was the 1990s when young, unknown comedians like Chris, Mike, and Tracy Morgan were performing on a regular basis at these clubs.

The Group had Wednesday night slots at *Carolines* with select nights at *Sweetwaters*. All of the comedians were starry-eyed and did as many gigs as they could, hoping for stardom. Daddy Leviathan was pushing for stardom as well. I'll never forget waiting in the back dressing room at *Carolines* with The Group's band members waiting to be called onstage and meeting a young Tracy Morgan stepping up to the mike and cracking his first joke, "Yeah that dude's gas smelled so bad, it was like an old man crawled up his butt and died!"

We all threw our heads back laughing not knowing he would move on to becoming one of the biggest comedians today. Anybody that follows Tracy's comedy knows his style of comedy has not changed. I remember stepping outside after a night of performing after Mike Epps delivered a side-splitting performance. During the performance, Daddy Leviathan was sitting at a table with his core groupie of women right in front of the stage. In the middle of his performance, Mike looked down from the stage at them and spontaneously said, "Oh yeah, he's fu_ __n' all of them!" The whole room roared in laughter.

I was amazed at how clear it was to folks on the outside what was going on while the secret was being hidden from The Group members on the inside. After Mike's performance and the show was over, I saw him outside standing nearby. I walked over to him and said, "You are really funny! You did great tonight."- Mike looked up at me with his big brown puppy eyes and then his head dropped. "But things aren't working out for me" he blurted out.

"Mike, you're extremely funny. I know you're going to be great!"

Well, as you know Mike Epps has gone on to do several movies, comedy, and television shows. Mike Epps is thriving today.

The Group also had gigs at *The Peppermint Lounge* in East Orange, New Jersey. Many of the Black musicians that were already featured on MTV and had radio airplay, hung out at *The Peppermint Lounge*. We met Queen Latifah, Naughty By Nature, Brian McKnight, and many others. These and many other clubs in the 1990s were where we showcased our music and Daddy Leviathan made a point to tell us that we were like Jesus hanging out with sinners in the clubs.

Daddy Leviathan introduced everyone in The Group to weed and alcohol some years into my time with them after graduating college. Daddy Leviathan and all of his "wives" smoked joints and drank beer or alcohol before every performance. Although I was quite eager, I could not smoke weed as much because I was not able to function after a few puffs. Plus, since I was not in his in-crowd of wives, I did not have the "honors" of joining them in their smoking parties.

The fact that we rubbed arms with so many folks who became famous, yet we experienced roadblocks and did not evolve lets me know God's anointing was not on us. In fact, I believe our music success was blocked by God. Daddy Leviathan did not deserve to become a widely known leader of the Faith because he was a liar, an adulterer, fornicator and encouraged all of his women to lie in his bed of sin with him.

In those early days, when I was not singing with the band as a background singer, I was assigned derogatory roles in the plays. Once I was given the part of a whore wearing a red dress handing out her phone number. Then I played a drunken washed-out bar singer that went to hell. The bar character was a famous singer who was self-centered and cruel. We did have a play called "Being In the House Versus Being in the Out House" and there was a scene in which a person was in the outhouse sitting on the toilet having a tough time. When they got up and left the toilet, my face was the prop above the toilet painted in white on the bathroom wall. During that scene, when the person saw me, we joined together and sang about having a heavy load!

I must say it was the funniest play we did, and I had a lot of fun. Yet looking back I cannot remember being in a role that was uplifting and positive. They preferred to typecast me in the lowest, and most demeaning roles. Others that were in his inner circle of groupies got popular roles like being an angel, preachers, teachers, or providing wisdom. These roles were reinforced in my brain to keep me down while feeling lost, defeated, and needy.

We were at an event at the Jacob Javits Center in New York to perform our hottest song, "Being Black." Daddy Leviathan spotted Spike Lee, who was blowing up at that time. This was right after his *School Dayz* movie. Daddy Leviathan had us walk up and sing the song acapella to Spike. During the song we began pointing people out, asking if they were Black. Our dancers also emphasized the question in their dance moves. Then Lucy would come in and rap about the true meaning of what it is to be Black which is not based on skin color. We all pointed our fingers right in Spike Lee's face.

Daddy Leviathan thought that Spike would be blown away with us and use our song for his next movie! Instead, we came across as abrasive and intimidating. I'll never forget Spike's long glaze, with those incredibly large, brooding eyes. He looked at us like we were crazy! When we were done, he just turned his back to us and calmly walked away.

We really believed that our music was going to hit the world and make a real change. We had the expectation of getting a big record deal, fame, and spreading the "gospel" through our great music. We were led to believe a record deal was going to happen any day. We hooked up with an ex-member of the group Slave and cut a deal with him to record our music.

A few of the members donated thousands of dollars for us to get custom original Mudcloth outfits for the record release party. We invited all of our friends and families to the record release party. After the event was over, the guy took our money and ran! We continued to pursue other avenues and did more studio recordings, but our music never went to the stratosphere as expected. Despite everything negative about The Group, our music was great! But now I clearly understand why God did not allow our music to get bigger, despite the great and uplifting songs we performed. Why would God want a liar and a pimp like Daddy Leviathan to represent him? And he said Christians were bad!

## Rough Riders

I think people would find it hard to believe that "Rough Riders" was my anthem song. In The Group they said we had to be warriors and soldiers for God and take the gospel to the world. Those words empowered me to take ministry to the lost. I listened to the censored version of DMX often. I related to his rapping about his anger. Unbeknownst to me at the time, I had a deeply rooted anger in me. Even Shirley noted that I like DMX because of him cussing folks out. She mentioned that I secretly wanted to do that to everyone in The Group. Well, I guess she was right! I suppressed my anger for 25 years! I felt like his rhymes were a release for me. I was the butt of jokes, chastised, and degraded. Listening to DMX, gave me my power back. No matter what the Elders or Elite of The Group said or did to me, DMX helped me cope.

In one of DMX's first albums, he talked about his grandmother praying for him. He talked about God a lot. I told The Group that DMX was going to get saved, and they laughed at me. I wasn't surprised when he gave his life to God in his later years. His passing left a void in my heart, knowing that he too, struggled in his relationship with God. RIP my brother.

# CHAPTER 13

# Forsake All Others

*"For whoever does the will of my Father in
heaven is my brother and sister and mother."*
**Matthew 12:50 (NIV)**

The Group used actual Scripture to twist it into their desired ulterior motive of absolute control. They used Matthew 12:50 to convince the saints to forsake everyone in their immediate family, extended family, and friends. No one mattered except the Elders and "saints" in The Group.

In Matthew 12:50, Jesus was responding to someone who informed Him that His mother and brothers were waiting outside to speak to Him. He asked the rhetorical question, "Who is My mother, and who are My brothers[1]?" Jesus was not being disrespectful to His family, but He was talking about those who believe in Him, and by believing in Him, they do what He asks, which is to do the will of the Father. In this way, you become His brother, sister, and mother.

The Group encouraged us to cut off our family at *all* costs. They will always defend themselves and say they never told us directly to cut off our families. However, this is a common tactic of cults. The goal is to keep you from connecting with anyone that will convince you to leave because an outsider's eyes are open to the cult's deceitfulness.

---

1 *Matthew 12:48*

I remember I was on fire for God after I got saved again by The Group. I came home and told my family what happened. I condemned them and told them they needed to get saved too. I did not feel that my family received my newfound self, so over time, I cut them off. I visited home less and less until I moved to New Jersey. I actually went years without going home to Long Island, and it broke my mother's heart.

At the beginning of joining The Group, the teaching was awesome to me. I prayed to God to teach me so that I could go into the world and preach the gospel of Jesus Christ and save souls. They ignited a fire for God in me, and I admired everyone that had the thirst for truth and righteousness. In reality, when you give yourself to God, He fills you with love and compassion, and He gives you the middle ground to reach out and help others. The Group preached over and over that cutting off your family is the ultimate sign that you have committed yourself wholly to God. They were so crafty with God's Word.

During my early years in The Group, my stepfather was on his deathbed, and I spoke to him. I asked him if he gave his life to God, and he defiantly turned his head away, as if to say, "Stop talking to me about these ridiculous things!" Looking back, I am wondering if I did all I could to help him embrace the love of God, as opposed to sounding like a cult recruiter. The Group's teachings used the Bible and made it so backward and selfish. There are several Scriptures that tell you to honor your mother and father, have no strife with your brother or family, and have love and compassion for your brother.[2]

The most ironic thing about The Group's insistence on forsaking your family is that *all* of the Elders in The Group were related or brought in other family members. Daddy Leviathan's wife and her twin sister were Elders. Shirley was Daddy Leviathan's sister-in-law, Shirley's sister, niece, and cousin were in the Elite Team as leaders. All of the leaders' 15 children were raised to believe they were

---

2  *1 John 4:20, Exodus 20:12, Matthew 19:19, Hebrews 10:24-25, 1 Peter 4:8-11, John 13:34-35,*

superior to all of the "saints." Here I was, walking into a family and extended family unit, and I was discouraged to communicate with and take care of my own family. Wow!

I was convinced this was the right thing to do. I cut my mother, sister, brothers, and stepfather off. I cut myself off from my family for 15 years. No Thanksgiving, Christmas, Easter, holidays, or birthdays. This was a personal decision, and no one outright threatened me or forbade me to communicate with my family. But the theme of giving your entire life over to Christ was wrapped over giving your life over to Daddy Leviathan and the Elders. They created a culture where it is expected to do as Christ did; see them as our mothers, brothers, and sisters whereby we cut off our "milk family," as they would use that term often.

I wanted to please God with everything I had, so I gave all of my financial resources, time, energy, blood, sweat, and tears to help build The Group, which became my family. Unbeknownst to me, I was actually helping to build a "milk" family whose leaders were rooted in evil. The following charts show the two main families whose leaders were running The Group. The charts also refer to incestual family relations that are discussed throughout this book.

# FAMILY INCEST TREES
## Shirley and Birdie (Sisters)

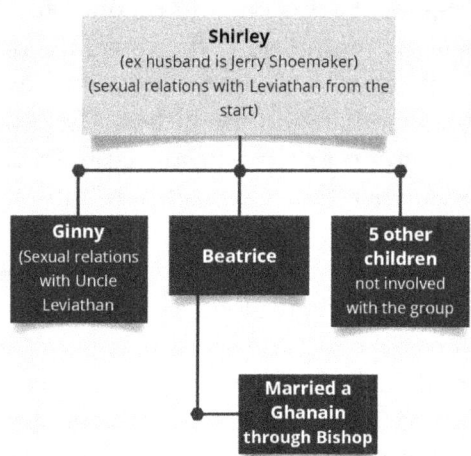

**Shirley**
(ex husband is Jerry Shoemaker)
(sexual relations with Leviathan from the start)

**Ginny**
(Sexual relations with Uncle Leviathan

**Beatrice**

**5 other children**
not involved with the group

**Married a Ghanain through Bishop**

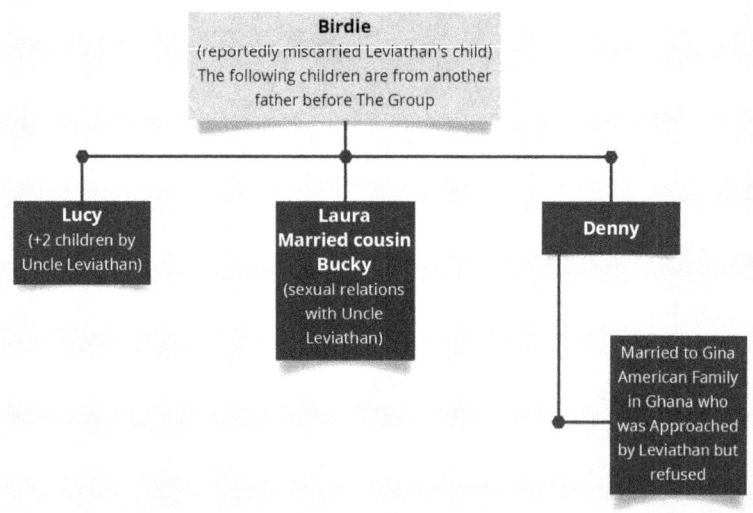

**Birdie**
(reportedly miscarried Leviathan's child)
The following children are from another father before The Group

**Lucy**
(+2 children by Uncle Leviathan)

**Laura Married cousin Bucky**
(sexual relations with Uncle Leviathan)

**Denny**

Married to Gina American Family in Ghana who was Approached by Leviathan but refused

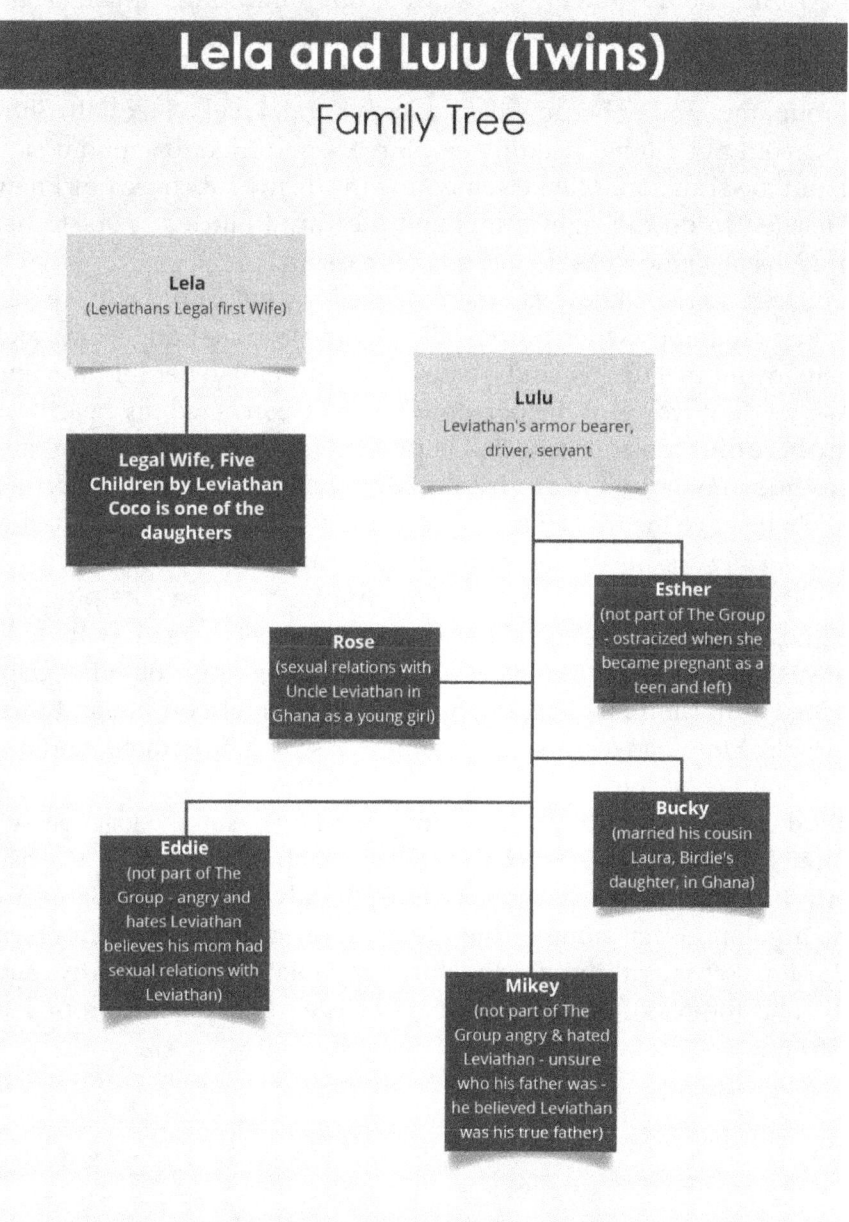

# Lela and Lulu (Twins)

## Family Tree

**Lela**
(Leviathans Legal first Wife)

**Lulu**
Leviathan's armor bearer, driver, servant

**Legal Wife, Five Children by Leviathan Coco is one of the daughters**

**Esther**
(not part of The Group - ostracized when she became pregnant as a teen and left)

**Rose**
(sexual relations with Uncle Leviathan in Ghana as a young girl)

**Bucky**
(married his cousin Laura, Birdie's daughter, in Ghana)

**Eddie**
(not part of The Group - angry and hates Leviathan believes his mom had sexual relations with Leviathan)

**Mikey**
(not part of The Group angry & hated Leviathan - unsure who his father was - he believed Leviathan was his true father)

As my mom began to age, I started communicating with her. I hated calling her because there was always a pull at my heartstrings—it's my mom, for goodness sake! About five years before I left the Group, my mother became ill and went blind. I had a talk with Shirley about my mother needing eye surgery and tried to sound casual about the situation. Maybe something inside my subconscious knew I needed to do the right thing, and the way I blurted it out to her must have sounded as if I lacked compassion.

Deep inside, I knew my mom needed my help, but I suppressed it. I was so happy when Shirley allowed me to go to Long Island and help my mom. For this kind gesture, I am grateful to her for directing me the right way. But the person who really convicted my heart was my beautiful cousin Michelle. I happened to arrive one day at moms on the same day she was visiting. Mom had become so fragile, and Michelle gave me this look, and without words, her eyes said to me, *You should be taking care of your mother.* It cut deep into my soul.

This initiated my visiting mom on a weekly basis, helping her bathe, manage her bills, and help my brother set things up with daily meals for her during the week. Then one thing after the other happened with Mom. In 2007 my mom's house caught on fire and then in 2008, Mom had a stroke. My mom was so sad, frustrated, and upset with me because she knew I was part of something that was not good for me. It was devastating for her all the years we lost contact. Mom lost me from 1989-2005! It was sheer abandonment. A warped mindset that kept me cut off from my family based upon Scripture manipulation that none of the Elders applied amongst themselves. But I'm so grateful that God restored my relationship with my family, and the restoration began years before my departure from The Group.

# CHAPTER 14

# The Illness of My Pain

*"One of the greatest tragedies in life is to lose your own sense of self and accept the version of you that is expected by everyone else."*
**K.L. Toth**

As the years waned on during my time in The Group, I developed several large fibroid tumors and I felt so unattractive. I was feeling more inferior to Daddy Leviathan's other wives who treated me like a servant. I was tall, and thin with a belly as if I was six months pregnant. I was in *Wholefoods* one day and a woman approached me and said, "How many months are you?" Shocked, I replied, "Oh no, I'm not pregnant. This is from an illness." She walked away red-faced and looked as if she was going to cry.

Over the years, I had internalized secrets, hurts, and pains for so long that I had fibroid surgery twice. The first one was in 2005 when doctors removed 50 fibroid tumors. My second surgery was in 2012 where 47 tumors were removed.

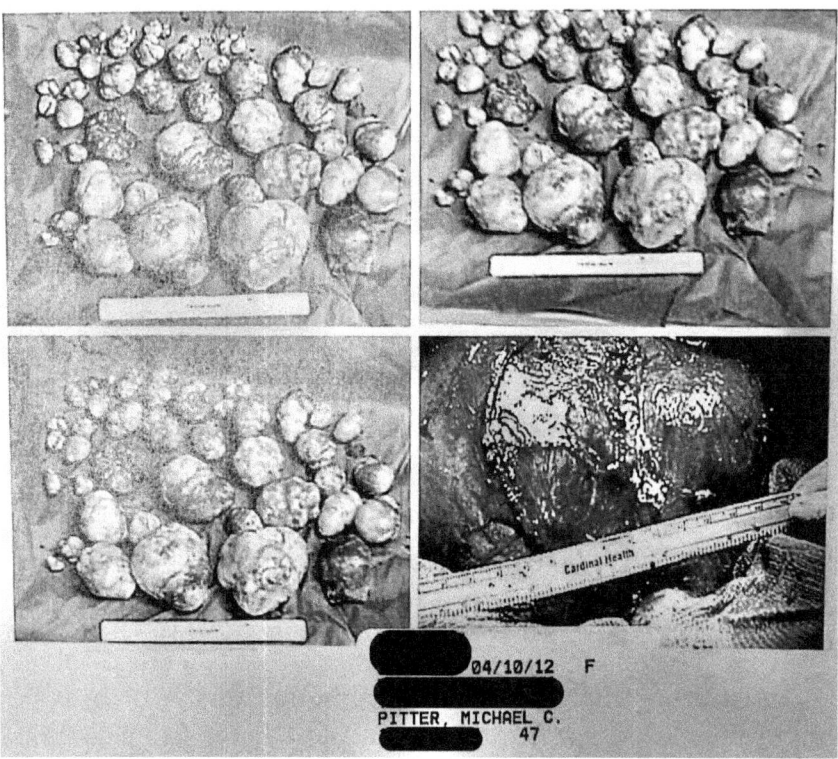

Both surgeries took many hours and it is a miracle doctors were able to preserve my uterus. I struggled between fighting thoughts of, *oh my God I have a rotten heart if I think Daddy Leviathan is a mean man and Shirley is mean as well. But they are my Elders and they hear from God.* I had no one to turn to. On top of that, I was getting in trouble in Bible class and if I made the slightest comment that went against the grain, I got shot down. I began to feel guilt and remorse for even allowing Daddy Leviathan to touch me. I felt angry that he did not honor me as a wife and didn't want to marry me. There were so many conflicting thoughts going through my mind.

Unbeknownst to me, internalizing so much hurt over the years was the source of my illness. Even though I was still healing from this first fibroid removal surgery, I made the trip to Ghana in 2005. I tried to see Daddy Leviathan several times and I was blocked and ignored. Shirley had offered me to stay in her room which would have been a great honor. However, one morning she busted the door open into the room unannounced. I was standing there in my underwear getting dressed for the day. I could tell she was angry. She had this look of privilege that let me know that I had no right to privacy. From her demeanor, I realized she regretted letting me stay in her room.

One day during that trip Shirley cooked a one-pot lunch and we all stood in line to be served by her. She had a spoon and happily scooped the meal from the pot to the plates. As soon as it was my turn, after serving about 7 people before me, she abruptly walked away. She loathed the idea of serving me! What a depressing trip. Being rejected by the two people I loved the most crushed me. I remember toward the end of that trip, I laid down in that room and I wanted to die. I was in bed all day. If I was able to commit suicide, I would have done it. That was one of the lowest points I have ever felt in my life. I uttered, "Lord I pray, take me. I want to die. I don't want to live anymore." That's how depressed I was.

## MARVELLA'S DIFFRACTION

All of the women who were thrown to the side outside of the walls of protection of his inner court were fresh meat for Shirley to publicly humiliate and get the rest of The Group to hate. I had already witnessed this with another sister, Marvella. But because we were convinced Marvella lost her mind in her own right, we were all warned to stay away from her. Marvella was obviously obsessed with Daddy Leviathan, demanding to be in the same car with him when they travel and live in the same room with him. Basically, she needed to be everywhere with him until she became so obsessive and demanding, he ran off and lived in the second home we provided for him.

Looking back, I see Marvella was driven to a state of anger and possibly insanity by Daddy Leviathan because of his abusive tactics. Marvella was an accomplished laser engineer who worked at Bell Laboratories. She had a Master's Degree in Engineering, concentrating on laser technology. She had such a brilliant mind, was also very athletic, and was an accomplished dancer, trained in ballet. She left her job at Bell Labs and moved to Ghana with Daddy Leviathan. They tried to convince her to stay in the U.S. because she was one of the biggest money-makers at the time. But her obsession with Daddy Leviathan got the best of her and she preferred to give up everything she worked so hard for in school and at work, to pursue the "ministry" with Daddy Leviathan.

However, once Daddy Leviathan physically separated himself from her, she finally left Ghana. I was secretly happy for her because it was evident, she was vexed while being with him. Shirley used Marvella to get sympathy from the congregation, propping up Daddy Leviathan as a man who can endure the sufferings of an evil, vexed wife. But in reality, she was another victim of wounded women that he used and rejected. Thankfully, Marvella eventually left The Group and returned to the U.S. to pursue a better life.

## Another Kick in the Gut

Five years later, I was still depressingly stuck in The Group. I was angry and confused that I had no final answer on the status of my relationship with Daddy Leviathan. I needed some type of closure or approval to move on with my life. I wondered, *Why would this man torture me when by now he had numerous wives*? There was a new member who was a younger, pretty sister who was being groomed to be his next wife. She was a successful veterinarian and he was courting her from Ghana remotely via telephone and video conferencing while she was in living in the house with the sisters in New Jersey. In 2010, I took another trip to Ghana as the "chaperone" for Daddy Leviathan's next main squeeze, Belle. Prior to the trip, I called and he said he was looking forward to seeing me. I told him I needed to talk to him.

Belle and I had a healthy, growing relationship while she lived with us at the house of women in Elizabeth until we had a run-in right before the trip to Ghana. I realized later what was happening. As soon as Daddy Leviathan began to court her, she began to be disrespectful towards me with smart-mouthed comments. Because I cherished our developing friendship, I did something I rarely did, which was to call her on it, telling her she was being disrespectful to me. I was hurt because we had such a great relationship. She was a former track star like myself, but she was a distance runner and could run for miles on end. She was not only beautiful on the outside, but she had such a beautiful soul until Daddy Leviathan got his influence on her. When a female is accepted into his inner circle, they are told they are better than everyone else. Then they begin to treat others as inferior. I never heard anything about my confrontation with Daddy Leviathan's future wife for the weeks that led to preparing for the trip.

The flight to Ghana from JFK is long—about 20 hours. But there was excitement with both of us as we got on the plane and finally arrived in the motherland. Lo and behold, as soon as we got off the plane and into the pickup van, one of the brothers picked us up and handed me the phone. It was Shirley. She stated, "I heard about what happened with you and Belle. Daddy Leviathan said don't mess with her and don't mess with his! Whatever happened between you and him is the past." *Wow*. I did not know how to respond.

They waited until I chaperoned her all the way to Ghana and as soon as we landed they cut me off. They just used me to make sure she arrived safely as Daddy Leviathan had his fangs out to dig deep into her neck and seal her fate with his venom. At the time I didn't have all of this wisdom. Instead of celebrating the fact that I wasn't his target, I felt a deep rejection and found it difficult to process that I was cut off.

When we arrived, Daddy Leviathan embraced her and did not acknowledge my presence. They both walked towards his living quarters. His other henchwoman, Lulu, looked at me and said, "What goes on behind closed doors between him and them is none of our business!" Yes, Belle was the new fresh bait. During that time, I thought Belle was the one that got the greater blessing because Daddy Leviathan welcomed her with open arms. They were going together everywhere, and she was staying with him in the same room. She was the prima donna and he brought out all of the tools to woo her silly. She was a smart, beautiful, educated woman that unfortunately got lured into his snare.

Ironically, I was in a private conversation with Shirley and one other sister, Dolores, shortly after the trip. Shirley slyly said, "I told

Belle to enjoy her honeymoon because it's not always going to be this way." I still remember the look she had on her face as if she wanted to break out in a hissing laugh. She knew Daddy Leviathan well. She watched him court, rape, rob, and throw beautiful young girls and women aside.

When Belle moved to Ghana and began seeing how things really worked, she spoke out openly about them. Since Daddy Leviathan was the prophet, no one could question anything he said or did. Less than two years after Belle joined herself to Daddy Leviathan, Belle gave birth to a daughter. She became one of Daddy Leviathan's most verbally abused and isolated women out of all of his "wives."

Belle was on the hot seat to be criticized. Shirley stepped in and convinced all of us that Belle lost her mind and suddenly became an evil vessel. It was like she was Marvella's replacement. We all drank that Kool-Aid and took the bait. Deep down in my heart, all I could remember was how pure and lovely Belle was while we were friends before Daddy Leviathan poisoned her.

I felt bad for Belle because she wanted to leave hundreds of times, but Daddy Leviathan would not let her take her baby. She ended up living in isolation and in her own personal hell for about 15 years. This is the treatment for women with babies by Daddy Leviathan who wanted to escape. He literally held your child hostage.

As I mentioned, Belle and I originally had a great relationship, but after she became Daddy Leviathan's new prize, we lost that bond. Not only that, I was also very hurt and rejected because Daddy Leviathan chose her over me.

# CHAPTER 15

# The Ostracized Wife

*"Deal with yourself as an individual worthy of respect and
make everyone else deal with you the same way."*
**Nikki Giovanni**

I felt so dejected and jealous over Belle's marriage and child with Daddy Leviathan. Little did I know that God was covering and protecting me all along. Once I left the Group a few years later, I connected with Belle, and our beautiful relationship was restored. She was finally able to leave with her child and move back to Seattle. She was open and willing to share her experience as one of Daddy Leviathan's wives in Ghana with me for this book. Here is Belle's story in her own words.

*My name is Belle. I am originally from Seattle, Washington. I met The Group when I was 19 years old in veterinary school at Washington State University. I was the only Black cohort in my veterinary classes. Yet there was another Black graduate student, Sharita, who was getting her pathology degree and a Ph.D. in another discipline. Sharita was from Philly. She became a big sister to me. One day she wanted to introduce me to her sisters in what she called "The Community." Throughout, they are also called "The Family" and "The Group."*

*These sisters came to visit her in Seattle. The first person she introduced me to was a woman named Donna. From time to time, I would hang out with Sharita, Donna, and a few other women from The Community. They* were all about ten years older than me. I thought it was grand because I was getting big sister support in a loving environment. My mother and I were not really close, and I had two brothers, so having a sisterhood was a new and fulfilling experience. When the sisters from New Jersey visited Sharita, I would go to her house for dinner. It was great to use my downtime with these ladies as an escape from the stress of graduate school. At the time, there were zero talks about religion.

Looking back, there were a couple of times when I was in the presence of the New Jersey sisters, like clockwork; one of them would make comments to another and say, "Doesn't she look like Jenny?" They would all nod their heads in agreement. It was weird how different sisters would say to me that I looked like someone else. Why do they keep saying that? What does that imply? I said to myself often. What struck me was that every time they made this comparison, there was a suspicious or somewhat taboo look between them in their eyes.

Fast forward two years later, as the youngest veterinary school graduate from Washington State University at 23 years old, I was already considering practicing on the East Coast. As a graduation gift, the sisters said they were going to send me a plane ticket to come to New Jersey. They were anxious for me to meet the rest of "The Family." I never got the free ticket, but I was planning to start a new chapter on the East Coast anyway. Little did I know that the sisters were grooming me to be one of Daddy Leviathan's wives. I fit all of the characteristics of his type of woman: tall, light-skinned, smart, and athletic.

The move to be near a sister connection like Sharita, my veterinarian classmate, was a no-brainer. I took a job in Baltimore in a small father-and-son veterinary practice. Some weekends I would just hop on Amtrak and visit Sharita and the sisters in Elizabeth. Again, there was no talk about religion. I viewed them as my friends and shopping buddies. Going to New Jersey was a nice place to get out on the weekends.

Early on, I may have stayed for Bible study once or twice in the Black House. I remember the Black House is where they always held Bible study. They also had another house in Newark and another house in Elizabeth where Anna and a few brothers and sisters lived. They were spread out between three different houses that The Family lived in, but normally when I came up to visit, I stayed at the red house on Union Avenue in Elizabeth.

*In hindsight, I tried to pinpoint events during that time that made me so vulnerable to The Group's tactics. First, I had a health scare. Then my best friend from veterinary school stopped speaking to me. I had no idea what had happened, but she was someone close, and we had so much in common. We both loved animals and were mixed Black women planning to relocate to the East Coast. Then my aunt died. On top of that, I had a bad romantic breakup with my boyfriend on the East Coast. That guy who broke up with me, along with my best friend, was part of the same friend group, so the loss was devastating.*

*I called Donna and told her what I was going through. She said, "Just come up here. It's going to be fine." So I started visiting New Jersey more often. That is how I began to transition and let my guard down. Life became so easy. It is so easy when you are going through something and have someone make decisions for you. There were constant conversations that ended with her saying, "Don't worry. We can go this way, or we can do that." I had no direction personally. I didn't even know where I wanted to live. That is how I ended up living with The Group.*

*I now had a big family of adults with kids. I loved the environment of being around a bunch of people and kids. Everyone was so kind to me. I didn't realize it was because I had favor with the Elite leaders as they were preparing me to meet Daddy Leviathan to be one of his wives.*

*Things at work in Baltimore began going downhill. I missed one day during a snowstorm, and the head veterinarian docked my pay. I had never called in sick and even worked when I had bronchitis and couldn't talk. I confronted him and told him that if he did not reimburse my money, I was done. With no job, I had thoughts of returning to Seattle since I was licensed there as well as in New York, Maryland, and Virginia.*

*I took a job as a relief veterinarian and worked a few days a month in Maryland. I wasn't stressed about money because all of my bills were paid, and since I did not have to pay rent in New Jersey, I was OK financially.*

## Searching For Enlightenment

*I was raised a Catholic, and my parents converted when I was three years old. I remember being baptized. As I got older, I was searching for something to fit me on the inside. I took a lot of Eastern Civilization classes and Eastern religion classes. I also read the Bible and the Quran. I was really searching* for spiritual wealth and warmth. But nothing set in because I would continuously see people say they are one thing from a religious standpoint and be pretty wicked.

One time we had Bible study at the red house where I was staying, and one of the Elders pointed to me and told me that I was saved. I didn't say no. Although I never really bought into the idea of being saved, I knew I would be considered rude or abrasive by my friends. I had just lost my best veterinarian friend, whom I considered family. The thought of losing this new family frightened me, so I went along with their program. After all, what was so wrong with living communally and supporting the family? I saw it as Black people finally supporting each other. I knew that the leader had kids and wives overseas, but that wasn't my business.

At that time, the mission was all about supporting the kids. I started sponsoring two or three of the youth in Ghana. I was buying their necessities. Being part of the bigger picture and larger purpose was important to me. I was looking for peace and contentment as I enjoyed living as a family. Then all of a sudden, there was an entire programming about your blood family versus your milk family. They talked about this separation from your blood family as a priority. This was a point they harped on. They basically programmed you to cut off your blood family, or else your life would be doomed, and you would be in sin. Then more and more rules for controlling your every move began to creep in.

When I returned to work, the Elders would say, "Belle, you cannot travel by yourself." They would warn me that bad things would happen to me if I traveled alone. The fear tactics were real. What if they are right? I thought. The Elders claimed it was for my safety. Whenever I had to catch a train, I would have to make sure someone picked me up on the way back. I don't drive—not even today.

I am a runner. I was a college athlete. I wanted to run a marathon, and I was training for it. Nobody in the household was fast enough to run with me, not even the men. I remember I got up and went running, and somebody who was adjacent to the community saw me coming back home and told on me. There was a very child-like tattling to the Elders by everyone who was not in an Elite class. My running became a huge ordeal. The Elders sat me down and chastised me about it. Then it became, OK, if you want to run, then Anna will run with you. But Anna couldn't keep up with me.

*Running became a big production. I would run, and someone would be driving behind me in a car. I was annoyed. Running was my peace. It was my calm. It was my medication. So I started manipulating the rules. I would go to work early so that I could run and then change when I got to work. They had no idea that I was running alone. Other times I would lie about when I was getting off work so I could run or do something personal.*

## Forbidden Videos

*I was told that Daddy Leviathan wanted to speak to me on the phone. I had never met him in person, and he was living in Ghana. The Elders and other sisters would make a big deal speaking to me excitedly, "He wants to talk to you! He's on the phone. He wants to say hi." Sisters would say to me, "That's crazy. You are so privileged." The entire group was hyped about me having a phone conversation with him. So the call happened, and it was nothing more than a how are you type of conversation.*

*Then one day, they were talking about Daddy Leviathan's birthday. His main henchwoman, Shirley, was talking to the sisters about making videos. Shirley pulled me aside and said he wants you to make a video for him of yourself. I responded, "OK." My first thoughts were that he wanted something like a day in the life of a veterinarian and wanted to know more about me. I quickly found out that was not what he wanted. Daddy Leviathan wanted women to make nude videos, and Shirley would send them to him.*

*There was so much community pressure. If you tried not to do it, Shirley found ways to get around it by saying, "If you are having a problem with the filming, I can have someone film it for you." I was still hesitant, and she said, "Go do this now!" It wasn't a choice. I made more than one video. Once I was standing, and another time, I was sitting. In hindsight, I realize that he was literally shopping for his next wife or plaything. That's the bottom line. I really felt like I had no choice: Do I want to stay in this community or be out? Nobody said no to Shirley. Since I was being chosen, it was seen as a privilege. Everyone aspired to move up the ranks or be chosen, and now, here is my chance.*

*There was always this type of manipulation that if you said no, what would the opposite be? I was never threatened. It was more like firsthand, you saw people who were not favored and you didn't want to be like that. They were treated lower. The kids would criticize them and make fun of* them. People would treat them almost like they had Leprosy. They didn't want to have anything to do with them. It was like that bad aura, and you really wanted to be favored.

The Bible studies were not really about the Bible. You just couldn't catch a break. Shirley, his right-hand woman would be so nasty and cutthroat to people. Always keeping people in place. Daddy Leviathan didn't manage anyone. The Elder women managed all of us. He had no power.

I will never forget Shirley saying, "He wants you to open up." So I opened up to some Scriptures that she directed me to. It was about going to a wedding. Later that day, I was on the phone with him, and he said, "What does that mean to you?" I don't recall the exact conversation back and forth, but I knew it was his way of pressuring me to decide if I was going to be one of his wives. I agreed to be a wife and move to Ghana and live with The Community.

Thinking back, when I was living in Ghana, and we had blow-out arguments about all of these other wives and the jockeying for position, it would frustrate me when I would call him a "bull crapper," and he would shout back, "I never chased any of these women. They always came to me!" That is what he would publicly say, and that is a bald-faced lie! Shirley and the other women in The Community groomed all of his wives as they were instructed to do so by him.

Fundamentally he is super aggressive with Shirley and the other females, including his daughter, towards them capturing women on his behalf. I found out later I literally look like Jenny. He has a taste. Just like Anna and myself, we are tall, light-skinned, and athletic. There is one of his wives that looks like me, and her kids look more like me than her! The women in The Community act as though they are getting bonus points for bringing in the women. That's how it came across to me in a dream. It was just a really crazy experience.

His eldest daughter, Coco, who I think is close to my age, would call me and other women with a similar pitch, "Bella I had this dream about you and my dad. You were holding this beautiful child." Coco is being raised up to be this perfect child, this example of great Godliness and love. She was grooming people for her father and yet taking friendships and bringing people in. Everybody wanted to be her friend because she was favored. There are two daughters from his first legal wife. One daughter was just completely *ignored, she was quiet, and this one, Coco, was given everything. So everyone chased after Coco to send money to support and get attention.*

*I reflect on my traumatic experiences in The Group often. I realized that I had to decide if I was doing something because I didn't want to rock a boat or if I was fine with it. I think about Shirley and the Elders control of me not traveling alone. I was caught up in fear. I remember traveling to Europe and New York alone before I met these people, and the anxiety and pressure were not there. By the time I met The Group, I was at a crossroads in my life after losing people close to me. I think that is what gave them such a level of control. If something bad happens to me, I am never going to hear the end of it. Almost like when your parents told you something and they were right.*

*What I realized is that silence was their power. People assume that we knew what else was going on with the wives and the misuse of the money being sent to Ghana for children and educational purposes. If I felt that there was any doubt that all these beautiful people that I had really loved since I was 19 years old, whatever they are doing must be OK because the people I care about are sanctioning it. There were countless times when I had an issue with something, but everyone else was fine. But then later find out that people didn't know the truth or people were willingly blind to remain part of The Family.*

*I know people don't like to hear the word "broken," but I think a lot of us today despise the thought of capitalism and the destruction of the family unit in Black and Brown communities, so we are susceptible to this type of family environment. It's no different than a gang. We all want to be part of a greater purpose. We believe in this greater purpose, this greater belief. It's not even about God. It's about supporting and living a life, especially outside of the U.S., racial discrimination and inequalities across the board.*

## The Chosen Wife

*I was escorted to Ghana to marry Daddy Leviathan by Anna. I got to know her more on the long plane ride. I saw how kind and intelligent she was. Shirley ordered her to bring me to Ghana and not talk too much because Anna was not privileged like me.*

*There was no official wedding per se. I don't know how it was for other people. Daddy Leviathan asked me to pick out a piece of jewelry. I selected a gold bracelet that was custom-made for me. I don't recall there being an official announcement. However, it was known that if a woman started dressing like him, then she must be one of his wives.*

*I was oblivious to the level of pedophilia and molestation that Daddy Leviathan went to get his wives. There were young women who were dropped off by family members in order to get an education, and they would end up pregnant. Girls who were not yet teenagers were groomed to perform sexual acts so as to not get pregnant. As soon as they became a little older, they ended up pregnant. Daddy Leviathan smoked weed and drank with these young girls to take advantage of them. Donors in the U.S. had no idea how much of their money was spent on jewelry, weed, and alcohol for Leviathan and all his wives and the Elders.*

*Daddy Leviathan had so many characteristics of a sociopath: charming, intelligent, lack of remorse, liar, narcissistic, spontaneous, and lack of love. Because of my constant questioning and not going along with the rules, I was ostracized. I was completely taboo in the community. Yet I was serving as the midwife throughout the community and in the area. I was putting in IVs and doing stitches. One of Leviathan's young wives' baby died, and they were hiding her pregnancy and the death from her family.*

*At that point, I knew it was toxic, I knew it was really bad, and I wanted to leave. To backtrack, I was never content or happy with anything The Group did in Africa, but I wanted to live in Africa to make a difference, so I have to claim my own accountability. Too many times, I was done with the U.S. way of life. From being around so many children, I wanted to have a child of my own. Maybe a child would give me the joy and fulfillment I needed. But I knew once I got pregnant with my hormonal changes, I would question the mission even more because what was the goal? None of these kids born and raised in Ghana even speak the language.*

*I was never sexually attracted to him, but I went along with the program. I only had one sexual interaction after I became pregnant. I told him, "Don't touch me. I'm good." Everyone was floored by how I spoke to him. I hated him. I didn't want anything from him. He focuses most of his time on sex. I think especially for young people. Every talk was about a young girl's body. He did not allow the men to masturbate because he said all of the releases were for him to do. He did not let girls and women trim their pubic hair. They did not want women to wear traditional bras. Only sports bras and oversized clothing. It was all about control. At this point, I had no desire to be the wife of this sex-crazed sociopath.*

## Sewing His Royal Oats

*It bothered me how everyone worshiped everything Daddy Leviathan said and did. No matter how much his actions were against the Bible, his hench-women would twist things and beef him up to be a God. I thought it was clever how everyone called him Daddy. Since he fathered so many children, no one would know which ones were his and which ones weren't. Only a few of us would be publicly acknowledged as one of his wives. A lot of the young children were never publicly acknowledged outside the household. It was crazy how people love titles, and they would do anything to interact with someone who had a title.*

*I was in a bad place mentally. My sister died, and then my father almost died six months prior. There was an Elder who was spoken very highly of by The Group. He came to visit Ghana. He was called The Bishop. I did not get to speak with him the first time he came to visit, but the second time, we hit it off because he reminded me of my dad, his presence, and his beard. It was just nice being around him.*

*I started witnessing things that didn't align with the Bible— complete-ly didn't align. I could see how everyone would be OK with multiple wives. Yet this man was with the mother and daughter. He has children with his niece. Once I found out about this, I really wanted to get my daughter out of there. I did not want to normalize this behavior. If you are sleeping with a mom, you cannot, at some point, sleep with her child. It's just wrong.*

*I kept finding passages in the Bible that did not add up. I spoke to The Bishop, and he agreed with me. He even wrote me a letter encouraging me to read the Bible for myself and pointing out that he did not agree with the happenings in the purple house, which is why he no longer visits.*

*The Bishop's words were encouraging. His words were confirmation that it wasn't just me and I wasn't crazy. I stood out as a troublemaker be-cause I was pushing against the grain of 70-plus people. Every time I spoke up about inconsistent words and actions, more and more people were told to stay away from me. It seemed when the truth was revealed to everyone by another person or circumstance, there would be "planters" to go around spreading things like The Bishop is jealous of Daddy because he wants to be like him and live this lavish life with all of these women. This was so far from the truth.*

*After having my daughter, I was sleep deprived for the first few years. I wanted him to take her for a few hours, so I could get some sleep. He never spent any time with his children. He pushed them off to the Elder women in The Community. I would argue with him and get loud, something no one had ever done. He wanted me to schedule a time to be with him physically, and I refused. I just wanted someone to come to grab my daughter for a few hours. I screamed, "Come get your kid!"*

*I remember one night saying to him, "I don't want to be here anymore." I threatened them. "I want to f'ing leave!"*

*"You can leave any time you want. But you can't take the kid!"*

*"You'd better let me take her because I'll report everybody here and let them know what you are doing."*

*I was mad and tired. I went to talk to Lela and Lulu, thinking these women, both mothers, would stand up for me and support my decision. The only thing they said was, "Well, it is his child. There is nothing we can do to help you." Their response was such a slap in the face. I thought. I must have really been out of my mind going to them in the first place. Lulu was his sister-in-law, and Lela was his real wife from New Jersey.*

*So from the time my daughter was two years old, I aggressively wanted to get out of that place. Maybe before two because I was still breastfeeding. I was in such a negative place. I had no help with my daughter, and I was tired, stressed, and almost suicidal. I needed rest. I would carry my daughter to the house and pound on the door. Oftentimes he would answer, and the room was filled with marijuana smoke. He smoked weed all day, which is illegal in Ghana. I would hand her over and say, "Watch her. This is your kid, she's your responsibility too."*

*I stopped going to Bible study because I realized that this religion that they speak of is bullcrap. I felt so isolated and alone because the two women who were like mother figures to me, now I didn't trust them. I started having anxiety because I believed they would take my kid and no one would help me. So I lived in fear for years that they were going to take her, so I always had to keep my eyes on her.*

*One day I had been thinking about my nude videos. I approached Daddy. "I want my videos now!"*

*I was getting loud. He went searching for them. He returned and handed them to me.*

"You will never use them to manipulate me like you manipulate everyone else." I tore them up in front of him.

I remember one of the young girls I was close to told me about the sex classes. Daddy would have his real wife, and her twin sister would have sex with him while the young girls watched. He would then have a young girl grab his penis and put it into the vagina of one of the women. It really made me start fearing the predatory nature of him as the father of my child. I was panicked if I couldn't find my daughter. Everyone called me crazy and told to stay away from me.

Then the Elders allowed me to be like the Auntie to everybody because I didn't want anything to do with Daddy Leviathan, but I love kids, so here's my purpose. I did movie nights, crafts, sewing, and homework help with the kids. They were still having many hours of prayers and Bible study every single day. I wasn't about that life, and they didn't want me there anyway because I would start questioning their views, and then it became an argument, and I often ended with "I don't agree with you on that." Basically, if you questioned what was being taught, you were publicly shamed, and you were frowned upon by everybody in The Community.

## Plans To Leave

When my daughter was around three years old I went to the Embassy with a makeshift birth certificate because she was born at home. I was crying hysterically and pleaded to the Black woman at the counter, "I have to get my daughter out of this country!"

"Unless the father signs this, you can't do anything!"

That was all she said, and she dismissed me. I realized then that I was f'ked. Daddy Leviathan would not sign the passport papers. I was living on this compound with financial dependency on them for everything: food, clothing, and anything I needed to survive. Around this time, others were getting passports for their kids. I said to myself, that is some bull. The Elders would claim that a family in the U.S. was paying for a kid's passport. I was livid. I told them, "I don't care if you can get a passport for these children you can get a passport for your daughter." Every day I was still fighting, still pushing. It was hard because whenever my daughter got sick, I did not sleep because I had no support. I was so sleep-deprived at times.

*Then I would start doing things like second-hand clothes shopping for the whole household, and I enjoyed it. I started engaging people on the outside because I am a very huge people person. Being around others who were not part of The Community gave me peace. On Sundays, I would go second-hand clothes shopping with 20 Ghanaian Cedi, which is the equivalent of $4 U.S. dollars. The clothes weren't for me. It was for people in the household, especially for the non-American kids and the non-favored American kids, because there was a huge dichotomy of who got what and who didn't.*

*I will never forget Daddy Leviathan was so delusional. He would approach me and try to talk to me, "How are you doing today?"*

*"Not good."*

*"Why?"*

*"Because I am being kept here against my will." I made sure I said this in public. He would just storm off.*

*I was chastised for speaking to Daddy like that in public, so they took the clothes-shopping experience away from me. I told them, "I didn't come to Africa to stay in the house!" I really wanted to be part of making a change in people's lives.*

*Not far from where we were, there was a little library owned by the fourth richest man in the country. He also has a hotel on the grounds. I started volunteering at the library doing story time reading in English. This is what I did at libraries when I was a kid, and that made me build a connection with others in a new circle.*

*Because of my volunteer work, I was invited to host programs at the hotel there, and from that, I was able to meet all the managers. I started riding horses and got connected to people of influence in the small town. It was great being around good, positive people. Even though I was not being paid, I was committed to my work. These influential people saw how dedicated I was to help others.*

*I started to have a life. I started to feel like I had a purpose. I was allowed to teach English at a small private school. One day I shared my story with the owner of the school. I told him how I could not leave to come back home to the U.S. without my kid. I was surprised by how these people were supportive of me. All along, I had been saying that silence was The Community's power. If no one ever speaks about the evil they do, then they will continue to do it.*

As I continued talking to the owner that day, he said, "Your daughter can go to school here. Don't worry about paying for anything." I was in shock. I was grateful that I didn't have to buy her a uniform. Everything was covered. So my daughter had a private school education for her last year while I taught English. She was around other kids in that environment, and she was happy.

Those in The Community were mad and jealous of her for going to this school. It was just wild. Then I started wearing clothes the way I wanted to wear my clothes. Everyone got to see me being happy and going against all that they warned about. I was enjoying my life. I had great friends. I was invited to amazing events for free. My daughter and I were having 5-Star hotel experiences because of my volunteer work.

I hosted national quiz competitions in the country. Life within The Community became progressively worse because they feared I shared their evil doings with my new friends. There were "planters" going around saying that I was wicked and crazy. They did everything to devalue my work outside The Community. Yet what they didn't know was that I got linked into this group with a Roman Catholic priest. The creepy thing is that this dude was a predator to me also. The good thing was that he connected me with a white Baptist man and his wife who lived in a huge house on top of a hill. I believe he was an aeronautical engineer who used to run an orphanage.

He assured me he would do what he could to get me and my daughter out of there. I actually had a fictitious birth certificate so another man could be the father. Ghana would not give me a birth certificate without a father's name, and the U.S. would not allow me to apply for a passport without the father's signature unless I had some huge documentation about why.

Around this time, I was asked to leave the big house in Bronybima and move to a smaller house. They made me move out two months before they actually left. As the truth about what they were about began to spread, they had to move to another city to re-tell the story.

My close friend from high school came to Ghana to help me get an appointment for my daughter's passport. Both parents had to be present. Daddy Leviathan said he would be there. So less than 24 hours before my scheduled appointment, I got this call from Shirley, his henchwoman, that

Daddy broke his leg and he can't come. I was so upset. I knew I couldn't trust them. I was determined not to miss this appointment, as it could be a long time before I got another one. I had the money from my friend, but I was willing to try anything to get this done.

I don't care if I was losing money because it cost around $400. So when I got there, I also had to prove that I was still an American citizen. My passport was not proof enough. The nasty Black woman from before wanted me to have a birth certificate.

"I've lived here for 15 years. All my stuff is gone, and I don't have access to it." Another white woman heard the conversation. She called me over to a private room. Thank God she lived in the Pacific Northwest. We had a conversation, and she asked me a few questions. She ended the conversation by saying, "I know you lived in America. I am going to just sign that off." Then she asks, "Do you have proof that she's your kid?" Ugh. Because my daughter was a home birth, the birth certificate was not enough. I had to do a DNA test that cost $700. My high school mate paid the $700 fee.

Lo and behold, a week or two later, Daddy Leviathan went to the Embassy and signed the additional paperwork. I think he was scared that I may have said something to the people at the Embassy. I finally received my daughter's passport. The Elders came and told me that they would save up for our ticket. I didn't say anything. I wasn't about to wait another two years or more for them to buy our tickets.

I never told them when I was leaving. I was very vague. A few days before we left, my daughter and I got a three-day all-inclusive stay at the luxury hotel. Nobody reached out to us. Nobody called to say goodbye. I made sure to let my daughter know that her father didn't pay for our tickets. I told her that people from the U.S. had sent the money. I didn't want her to buy into the myth that he is this perfect man. Then I realize that he doesn't love anybody but himself because he's setting his kids up for no future. Not one of them is a functioning adult. The older ones have never had jobs. They are living off others from the U.S.

I was so anxious to get on the plane. As we were on the way to the airport, the Elders called us. They wanted to speak to my daughter. "No! Where were you these past six or seven months while we were living in the house? You had no interaction with her."

*So they continue to tell stories and paint false images and lies. They tell people that they support me in the U.S. I don't get support. My daughter needed a laptop for school, and they sent it along with a $100 GAP gift card. For the first few months, I had to fight them and demand that they do more. I became angry and bitter. I realized that being angry at them made me their slave. So I let go of that anger. Now, if I ask for things for my daughter, they can choose to help out or not. I have zero expectations from them. I am grateful to live in the State of Washington, where I get free medical, dental, and vision for both me and my daughter. If I wanted to take him for child support, the State of Washington would take his passport because he owes back pay. I decided that I won't let my child engage with any of them.*

*When this story comes out, my daughter will be 13 years old. We arrived in Seattle when she was ten and a half years old during the COVID-19 pandemic, so she is now learning to interact with American teenagers. Her grades are great, and we are taking it one day at a time.*

*I have a great job as a community builder and leader for the largest housing organization in the state. What I love most about my job is that I get paid to be who I am. I know and love myself. I also know the feeling of being alone and not knowing about resources is what drives and pushes me to want to support others. I help people feel a sense of community and less loneliness, which makes people less susceptible to manipulation.*

*The weird thing is that the longer I am back in the U.S., the harder it is for me to share with people what I've been through. The thing is, there should be no shame. It's my experience. Unfortunately, the narrative that is put on women is that we are stupid. We are not stupid. We are lost and lack connection to other humans. I imagine if Anna had a better connection with her father, she would not have been susceptible to The Group. If I had a better connection to my mother, maybe I would not have been a part of The Group either.*

*I am also a mindfulness instructor now. Although people pretend they are not herd animals and don't need other humans, it's unrealistic. We are made to be connected to one another. It's how we are designed.*

*There is always a dichotomy in my experiences with The Group. In spite of 15 years of mental abuse, there's a joy about it that I miss because I had a life outside the household. I made friends with people in those last couple of years in Ghana that are closer than any friends I have of 25 years.*

*There are places of peace and real conversations about life, and work, not about how much you make. If I sit and think about how much money I lost in income, that alone would floor me. It would be on the scale of millions.*

*As I look back, I think they were foolish. Poor planning in their organization. If they wanted me to stay in Ghana, it would be more beneficial if I came and went. They didn't even have that long-term goal. Even towards the end of my stay in Ghana, I didn't have food. There was a huge food shortage. We were living in Ghana and ate mostly American food, which was very expensive: baked chicken, collard greens, rice, and macaroni and cheese. First, everyone got three meals a day, then it became two meals a day. Then it became one meal a day for adults, and the kids could get something in the morning. Yet Daddy Leviathan and his other wives got three meals a day. What man doesn't make sure his kids eat first?*

*There are days when I think about my experiences in The Group and remember the anxiety that overcame me when I thought about two outcomes of living with them in the house at Bronybima: 1) It would be another Jim Jones tragedy because, at a certain point, the followers would realize that whatever Daddy Leviathan is talking about is not happening or 2) Daddy Leviathan and a couple of his wives are just going to get up and disappear one day.*

*The Community as a whole is a bully. I believe that if you speak your truth and your experience, how can that be something wrong? The Group does not have the power or the resources that many people think they have. I am now in a greater place on so many levels. Despite everything that I have been through in the past 15 years, I have peace and joy, and more importantly, I still have my mind. If anyone in The Group reads this story, please know that I don't hold any ill will or grudges toward you. I don't have to because karma is a b\*tch!*

# CHAPTER 16

# THE CLEAN-UP WOMAN

*"There is no worse evil than a bad woman; and nothing
has ever been produced better than a good one."*
**Euripides**

The devil always needs an accomplice. When I think about the relationship between Shirley and Daddy Leviathan and how he used her to groom, bait, recruit, and sexually abuse women, I cannot help but compare similarities of my experiences and those of other women in The Group with the Nxivm Sex Cult case. I can clearly equate Shirley's role as an Elder to Allison Mack, the *Smallville* actress who recruited women on behalf of the cult leader, Keith Raniere.

Evil men have a charismatic way of manipulating and using women they have had sexual relations with to prey upon and commit terrible acts upon other women. Raniere used self-improvement, and Daddy Leviathan used Scripture and educating young people. Raniere received 120 years in prison, while Allison Mack will go to jail for three years. God will judge the Elders of The Group and all of the imps that carry out Daddy Leviathan's perverted and criminal purposes.

That night when Shirley grabbed me by the waist and hugged me as I was trying to leave the first Bible study, I felt like I bonded with a woman for the first time in my life. Since I was used to having a mother figure, it seemed like that was what I needed as a college student away from home. I can honestly say that her embrace was one of the most beautiful moments of my life—someone showing me love. I actually felt love, so I believed that Shirley loved me.

I was glad when my friend invited me to Bible study for the first time because I wanted to be part of a church. I was convicted because I had sex with my boyfriends while in Farmingdale. I was raised that sex before marriage was a sin. I wanted to be right with God, so I believed it was time to fix my soul because I had backslid.

All of my encounters with Shirley were never about me submitting myself to God. Instead, it was about submitting myself to the Elders and believing that they were put into place by God to watch over me and teach me how to live. In theory, it made sense that God has trusted individuals to mentor and provide guidance, but not to control you.

## The Queen Mother

Shirley was Daddy Leviathan's, right-hand man. She was second-in-command. Whenever he was not present, she taught the class and had full authority and reign over us. She was regarded as the Queen and the Mother of The Group. When I graduated I moved into the two-family house with Daddy Leviathan, his wife Lela, and their five children. On the left side of the house were Shirley and her husband and their seven kids.

Shirley's husband was the brother of Daddy Leviathan's wife, Lela. As a college graduate with an electrical engineering degree, I was relegated to sleeping on the floor behind a couch in the living room. Daddy Leviathan's wife Lela wanted me to live with them, but I did not realize until I arrived that they did not have a bedroom or furniture for me. So I used the large suitcase I arrived with for my books and other belongings, and cleaned out used crates from the local supermarket dumpster to store my belongings behind the couch. The house was large, old, and damp. There were roaches and sometimes mice running rampant day and night.

I was unemployed for nearly two years, and I slept on the floor with minimal belongings throughout that time. By then, Daddy Leviathan had multiple other women, so he moved into the basement of the house with his women, while his wife Lela and I remained on the first floor with the children. Shirley and her husband were separated because he found out (unbeknownst to us at that time) that Shirley had been sleeping with Daddy Leviathan, her brother-in-law. That truth was held from the congregation. Instead, we were led to believe that Shirley's husband was a madman, an enemy of the Elders.

Daddy Leviathan praised Shirley for having the gift of revelation and knowing everyone's faults. She walked around like she was superior and was very judgmental. I didn't feel comfortable around her, **ever**. One time during Bible study, she said, "Oh yeah, and I can read your minds. God has given me the gift of knowing what you're thinking. I know what some of you are thinking right now!"

Then she would say something really harsh and proclaim that condemnation would come down at that moment. She was using the fear tactic. Fear is a common way to keep people down. When she said this, it terrified me. I began to develop a fear of her and feel inferior in her presence. That's the way it was designed, and it was working.

One afternoon, while living in the two-family house, I heard Shirley screaming at the top of her lungs. I was startled. She was having an argument with her ex-husband. She shouted, "You raped me! You know you raped me! Your last child was a child conceived out of rape!" I was shocked. I had no idea she was having these types of deeply rooted marital issues. Her ex-husband was living with her and the five kids in the house because, although they were divorced, she had nowhere else to go.

I felt sorry for her. I thought of how my mom was abused and my maternal instincts kicked in and I had to do something to get her and the children out of that house. After I heard the argument, the next morning, Shirley, her kids, and Daddy Leviathan's kids were in the kitchen. I burst out, "I'm going to get you a house!" Well, they all laughed, but it was one of those "oh how sweet of her" laughs, or like "she is dreaming" kind of laughs. At the time, I was volunteering as a teacher at The Group's Christian homeschool with no pay, so I had no money.

I was part of the staff that taught all 17 children of the Elders and their cousin's children. I remember putting cardboard in the bottom of my shoes because I had worn out the bottom of my soles walking to and from the school. Not long after I spoke that word in the kitchen, God blessed me with a great job as an engineer at the Princeton Plasma Physics Laboratory (PPPL). It was my first real good job since graduating from college two years prior, and God has continued to bless me ever since. My experience at that job was surreal because of my love for physics. I frequently gave tours to students of the Tokamak Fusion Reactor and attended educational colloquiums given by Princeton Physics graduate students. I still remember attending an event by then post-graduate, Dr. Neil deGrasse Tyson, and I was fascinated by his presentation on astrophysics theories.

The moment I heard him speak, I knew he was pure genius and on his way to greatness. I was so proud that he was a man of color giving young children inspiration and hope just by being who he is. Although I was estranged from my mother since graduation, I told her the great news of getting my dream job at PPPL. She offered me a gift of love: a used gray Nissan Sentra stick shift. My stepfather bought it for her, but she didn't know how to drive it. One of the sisters in The Group, Jessica (Jenny's older sister), taught me how to drive the stick shift. It was the best experience we had together. But since she was one of Daddy Leviathan's main wives, I was not good enough to be friends with her. Nevertheless, I was grateful that the car lasted me for a year. But then my car broke down. I took the train to and from work and saw Dr. deGrasse on the New Jersey Transit Trenton train a few times. We engaged in conversations about God. He made his beliefs clear, but on one trip I gave him a cassette recording of our music and invited him to see us perform in New York City. Again, I was never confrontational with anyone that I would discuss the topic of God, unlike The Group's tactics, so people have and still find me to be very approachable and engaging.

Dr. deGrasse came to our performance with his wife and enjoyed the show! About 10 years later, I reached out to him to request a tour of the Hayden Planetarium for my students, since he became the Director. By then, after I got home from work, I was teaching the home-schooled students science. I was so honored that not only did he give us free tickets for the tour, but he gave my students a special 1-hour teaching session just for us. By this time, he had already gained prominence in the world of astrophysics. My students knew who he was, and they were very excited. God always found a way to bless me, despite the haters.

When I got that job, I used my first paycheck to grab Shirley and her seven children and rented a home for them in Elizabeth to get her away from her ex-husband. Although they were divorced, she had no financial means to move out. I felt honored to be the one to give her peace and solace away from him and help her and her children have a fresh new start. It was a nice quiet neighborhood. Prior to the move, Shirley and I had a student-teacher relationship. Every time I would see her it was just strange. I felt like I was under a microscope. *Was she really reading my mind?* I believed we were off to a great start and I was getting to know her and the family. We even got a beautiful Chow Chow named Diablo.

In The Group's early days, when they were under Ma Shoemaker, Shirley was Daddy Leviathan's first infidelity once the two families moved in together. She was also the first to get kicked to the curb. Shirley was definitely scorned and masked her pain. She was convinced that despite all of his other "wives" that he loved her more than anyone else. Although the relationship became strained when she realized I was a "spiritual" wife, we found a way to coexist in the same house since I had my own room, and I worked during the day. There was still Bible study six days a week in the evenings where she would lead and teach after Daddy Leviathan moved to Ghana.

I began to see Shirley's true personality in full bloom in the mid-1990s when we traveled to clubs, schools, and churches performing music, plays, and skits, prior to the Ghana exodus. She and the Elder twins Lulu and Lela would meet up at a bar for drinks after the performances. One time she took me along as a privileged guest, so I thought. In essence, I was being set up for a kill. After she had a few drinks, she started spilling Daddy Leviathan's secrets to me.

I told her my secret that I was feeling rejected by Daddy Leviathan because he was not honoring me and bringing me into his inner circle like the other wives. Looking back, I realize that up to this point, she didn't know about my sexual encounter with him. I told her that I was sad because he just left me like I was not worth the time of day. She replied, "Well listen here. He took me four years ago and hasn't touched me since then! But trust me, he'll never love you the way he loves me. And he'll never love any of those other girls the way he loves me. I am the true queen in his life." She said this straight from her mouth to my ears!

Her voice grew firm with a confrontational tone. I wasn't a fighter and I definitely was not going to fight over a man— never have and never will. She basically wanted to fight that night, but I was not going to be pulled into her pain. I often wish that I had the clarity back then to see how crazy this was. Shirley gave up her marriage for Daddy Leviathan, and he flaunted his women around her and had her do his dirty work. If there's one thing Shirley got right in our conversation about Leviathan is that their connection was stronger than any other connection he had with other women—even his wife.

No other Elder carried the power and weight of Shirley. Daddy Leviathan was number one and she was hands down, number two. I believe having so much power over others is what kept her going. Yes, she was hurt and dejected by him, but he publicly put her on a pedestal that no one else could claim. After my confrontation with Shirley in the bar that night, our relationship deteriorated. She made a point of going out of her way to belittle me for everything that came to her mind. She even allowed her kids to disrespect and belittle me. One time I raised up enough courage and told her that they needed to respect me. She said, "No, you don't need to be respected."

As the years went on living in the house with Shirley and her kids, my depression grew stronger and stronger. My demeanor was noticeable to everyone and I could not hide my pain. I was no longer happy on the inside or outside. We were taught that if you are free from sin you are God's gift and that means you are projecting the best on Earth: happiness, love, and compassion. So if you were not happy, you were in sin and condemned to hell and they sure made you feel like that in their actions as they made you feel like you were the lowest person on Earth. There was no room for suffering from depression—that was considered an outright sin.

People whispered that I had issues. I stood out like a sore thumb. I was angry that Shirley was never the mother figure I thought she was. She never had the love or compassion to help me heal. I had this pain in my soul about this man having sexual relations with me and leaving me hanging with no marriage or any contact. There was no honor in what Daddy Leviathan did to me. I felt dirty and kept so much inside that the uterine fibroids illness was a manifestation of my pain and frustration.

As time went on, I was becoming delusional. I wanted to be in Shirley and Daddy Leviathan's inner circle badly. I needed to be accepted. I needed to know I was in right standing with God because they represent God on Earth. Daddy Leviathan always said, "If you're good with me, you're good with God." I wanted to be the epitome of being good with God. I wanted to be good with Daddy Leviathan and I was jealous of the women who got to spend 24 hours a day 7 days a week with him. None of them worked and they just laid around in luxury and traveled with him.

After two years, we had outgrown the house in Elizabeth. I then moved Shirley and her family into a bigger three-story house in Newark. We needed to have rooms for the five kids as they continued to grow. In spite of the uncertainty and confusion in my personal life, my career took off. God was blessing me in the corporate world and I was earning six figures and receiving promotions often.

Shirley went out of her way to destroy relationships I had with others. She first began doing this with the children. When the children became teenagers they formed a band. As I mentioned, The Group put on plays and musical events often, and when Daddy Leviathan and his chosen women left for Ghana, the children, picked up the instruments they left behind and began to play. I thought the kids sounded great! I helped them with their original songs by working with the singers in the band, teaching them harmony and how to hold notes. I enjoyed working with the kids as it was a refuge from the tensions of living in the same house with Shirley and being on edge during Bible studies.

I made my first trip to Ghana in 1997 when Shirley and her kids lived with me in Newark. I remember to this day when I arrived. It was a clear situation of "us" vs "them." I entered the gate of their home in Accra and one of Daddy Leviathan's wives, Jessica, looked at me and rolled her eyes. Jessica and her sister Jenny were part of Daddy Leviathan's inner core of wives. She would always find the chance to put me down. Looking back, I see that she saw me as a threat. I had such low self-esteem, that I did not see myself as beautiful. But on the outward, I definitely had a big advantage. Her sister Jenny ended up becoming the prime wife. They were both tall and light-skinned. Jenny had long, straight hair and made it known to everyone by her actions that she was highly favored. Most of the wives in Daddy's inner core spent their sacred energy vying for position with him. Although I was financially supporting them, they put me to work to serve them popcorn and do menial things while they sat in the presence of Daddy Leviathan all day.

## Lies and Confrontation

While I was there, I found out that Daddy Leviathan told Shirley I said that the kids don't rehearse their music. I was totally thrown a curveball because I don't recall speaking about the kids and music while I was there. If I did mention them it would never be anything negative because I really loved them. False words got back to the kids about me and it broke their hearts.

The confrontation started the moment I arrived back in Newark airport from Ghana. Someone from The Group was supposed to pick me up from the airport. After I retrieved my luggage I looked around and my ride was not there, so I went to a phone booth and called the person who was supposed to pick me up. I was told to wait and that someone was on their way. There were no bad words or confrontation, I just needed to touch base because I was at the airport alone with no one to greet me when I arrived.

That night at Bible study, Shirley began an immediate confrontation and blurted out, "Oh and here she is coming back from Ghana. She was in the presence of the holy of holies, the king, and prophet of God. But as soon as she gets off the plane she's calling and rushing for somebody to come pick her up. They were on their way already and she just had to make a phone call asking who is picking me up and where is my ride?"

I was in shock that she began to attack me right out the gate publicly. The Elders pushed the notion that when you are in the presence of Daddy Leviathan you're basically in the presence of God and it's expected that when you go to Ghana, you come back on a higher spiritual level. Shirley put on an all-out hate campaign against me as soon as I stepped in the front door.

I was depleted and I apologized to The Group. I was also crushed by the lies they said I made about the kids. I used my three-week vacation to visit Africa for the first time and I had these huge hopes and dreams of my future in the education ministry and how I could help the people. Instead, I walked into a witch hunt. I was looking forward to Bible study because I wanted to testify about the good things that were happening in Ghana and she ruined it. Now that Daddy Leviathan was in Ghana with his women, Shirley was in charge. She was evil and more wicked than ever before.

To make matters worse, she had the rest of the congregation behind her. So all of her negative disposition towards me gave others the green light to talk down to me and treat me poorly. I'm not the only person that this happened to, as there were a handful of other women—Daddy Leviathan's rejects like me who received harsh treatment. Fear of going to hell and wanting redemption kept us all locked in. We did not dare to even think about leaving, since we were brainwashed to believe doom and damnation awaited us like all of the other folks who left.

Years later, Shirley moved into the Black House that Daddy Leviathan and his harem used to live in prior to his departure to Ghana. I lived nearby down the street. The Black House is where we had Bible study six days a week. Our only day off was Saturday. One Sunday we were having Bible study and Shirley let her daughter Ginny conduct the lesson. It was a series of direct attacks on a few people in The Group. Whoever leads Bible study is allowed to rule over everyone else.

## Hell Nights

On this day, her daughter wrote out a note in pencil that she wanted me and three other women to sign stating that we are waiving any legal ramifications for anything that was going to happen in the Bible study. I was taken aback as to why she wanted me to sign this piece of paper. It was so unprofessional and written in pencil on line-ruled paper. But I went ahead and signed it because even though I hated my situation, I still had deep trust for Shirley as an Elder. Later that night when the four of us women walked into the room, the men of The Group had a large wooden paddle with holes drilled into it. Drilled holes were there so that when you got hit by that paddle, you'd feel the most force. We were told off about how we were not walking right in the Lord. Then we were ordered to line up to be beaten. Some of us got light hits, some got it bad.

When it was my turn to get hit, the brothers were so excited to hit me. I could see Shirley's henchmen Kaarme's devilish smile waiting for his turn. Then Jim, a 6 foot 3 married brother who had been trying to get in my pants, was the first to hit me with full force. Then the rest followed. I was in so much pain. My butt was black and blue for at least three days. I recall standing at my desk at work for the entire three days because it hurt so bad to sit down. At that time, there were no cell phones to take photos, and it did not cross my mind to report them. I was still loyal to The Group. This was the lowest of the low in my experience with the congregation.

I was in such a depressed state, I didn't know what was going on. Maybe they were trying to beat the depression out of me. After I left The Group I prayed to God to ask what I did to deserve something as horrible as this whipping. I have gone over and over in my mind and the answer I always got was that I did not do anything to deserve such physical abuse. The physical abuse was also mentally crushing since I was a provider for Shirley and her children. I paid rent, and as many bills as I could, and I learned to curb my smart mouth. Nothing I did was ever good enough.

After that whipping, I was so depressed that one day I just dressed up like a clown and bought some tin pans and filled them with whip cream pies and just let everyone take a pie and throw it at me. I was going through different levels of depression and had a deeply-rooted subconscious fear of something happening or something being said to me. So instead of them hitting me first with their harsh words, I thought maybe I could have a little power over what happens to me. I handed pans of whip cream out to everybody and they were all down to throw it in my face. Later, Shirley's daughter told me that I hurt Shirley's feelings because she said, "Oh, that's what Anna thinks of us? We're abusers to her?"

Shirley always found a way to humiliate and embarrass me. Years prior to Daddy Leviathan's departure to Ghana, Shirley was leading a Bible study in his place. During the Bible study, she implied that I said or I did something wrong. I had no idea what she was talking about. She had the congregation form a circle around me as I stood in the middle of the room and gave everyone a chance to tell me off. One by one each person said something that was just breaking my heart. I finally fell to the ground yelling and begging for forgiveness from God and repented for any and every thing I was accused of doing.

The room went quiet. No one forgave me. I remember when I got home, I went into my room and stood in the mirror. I felt God's strength and I felt Him in my heart. I heard Him say, "Look at you. You're my beautiful daughter." Instantly, the pain in my heart was removed and I was able to shake off that experience so that I was able to get up the next day. That night was so bad that even Daddy Leviathan scolded the congregation the next day for how they treated me. He secretly told me Shirley lacks judgment. But he never openly scolded the henchwoman that drove everyone into the hate feast.

Another mob night happened after my first fibroid removal surgery in 2005. I had twelve stitches on my belly where the doctors removed 50 tumors. I could barely walk and I lost a lot of weight. At that time I was living in the house of women and two men in Elizabeth. The sisters said they would take turns caring for me after my surgery since I couldn't go up and down the stairs to eat. I was to stay off my feet for six weeks. So the first two weeks I really couldn't move around at all and a few sisters volunteered to take the day off from work to help me. This was the time Belle was in favor with Daddy Leviathan since she was in line to be his next wife, she got on the phone with him complaining about me.

After a few weeks, I was able to get out of bed and go to Bible study at the Black House. I was excited to testify about how God protected me and how I could have died on the operating table from my surgery because I lost a lot of blood. Instead, they planned to have the children put on a play so I could not testify. As their play continued, I realized that they were making fun of me by doing a re-enactment of me asking for the sisters to get me something to eat. At one point, one child was pretending to be in bed and asked someone to bring her a hamburger. Then the person in bed asked for ketchup. They made it seem like I was driving the sisters in the house crazy and everyone was laughing.

The skit was very funny and I was laughing too because I really thought it was done in light humor and I was just so happy to make it out of that surgery whole and I did not need a hysterectomy. However, within a few moments, it turned into a mob gang with Shirley leading, complaining how Belle took the only day off she had, and I was asking her to do things for me. I still had stitches in my stomach and was in pain. Instead of them talking to me about it privately, Shirley complained about me openly. I literally again fell to the ground on my knees saying, "I'm sorry! I'm sorry. Please forgive me!" The more I showed love and compassion for others in The Group, the more I was treated less than human.

Shirley and I visited Ghana together about three months after my surgery in 2005. When we got to the airport there was an issue with her ticket and she was getting an attitude with the attendant. Here I was with my "sinless" leader who was trying to check the airport attendant. I took note of her behavior because she was really out of line. We were able to board because we had to pay a few hundred dollars more for her ticket. As we were boarding, I verbally blessed the pilots and wished them a good and safe flight. I lightheartedly told them to bring us there safely.

Once we arrived in Ghana and went to Bible study, she immediately testified as to how God delivered her regarding the issues with the plane ticket and the Lord delivered her from it all. I was shocked. All we had to do was pay more money and she was livid with the attendant. She also left out the part about her behavior. Nevertheless, I felt *let me keep it on a light note* and so I chimed in saying how I blessed the pilots. Her demeanor immediately changed. She began to belittle me and say I had no power to bless anybody and to stop trying to jump into her story.

What's ironic about that moment is that as she spoke she had on these large $200 hoop gold earrings I paid for that were dangling and chiming as she moved her head. I financed most of Shirley's clothing and jewelry as I provided money to the sisters in Ghana to buy her beautiful clothes. She also had this $300 large leather designer gold metallic purse that I bought for her. I was so mentally depressed that she could trash talk me in front of everyone, insult me, and I had to be quiet. I bought her expensive sheets, comforter sets, pillows, and accessories for her room. But as she made that comment to me, I did have a small awakening and for a moment, I saw the evil inside of her.

I didn't say anything to her because I was trained to "cast the imagination out of my head because she is my Elder." I just cowered in my seat in front of everyone including the new Ghanaians that I was to meet. I didn't have a chance to build any meaningful relationships with many of them because she made sure to openly tear me down.

Daddy Leviathan always made sure to tell us that we needed to take care of the Queen Mother, "She should never have to pick up anything off the floor," were words he said often. There was a girl who cleaned her room in Newark at the Black House that left The Group. Then I had to clean her room for a few years. It was pure torture cleaning up after her as I had seen her true colors. Whatever I did for Shirley, I just had to tell myself the Scripture, "*Whatsoever you do, you do unto the Lord.*"

Another incident with Shirley that sticks out in my mind happened around December 2006. I was starting a new job in New York and there was a girl named Michelle who worked in the IT department. She was having personal issues and one time she fainted at work right by my desk. As I came to her aide, she confided in me that she was depressed. She was really drawn to me, and we had discussions about God and salvation. One day I invited her to Bible study to bring her to Shirley, a great teacher who I believed could get her on the right track. As you can see, this shows my state of mind. I was programmed to believe that I could not be a source of hope to anyone. Only the "sinless" Elders could fulfill that role or those that they give favor to in the congregation. Michelle followed me from my job to the Black House. It took almost two hours to get from work to the house as there was a ton of traffic. That should have been an omen to me the night was not going to go well.

I had bought cheese and crackers to have snacks before class. My heart was really happy because I wanted my great teacher and mentor Shirley to meet Michelle and I knew she was going to be blessed. When we arrived, I told Michelle to go into the living room and I was in the kitchen with the sisters preparing the cheese and crackers platter. I noticed Shirley was not supportive of what I was doing and thought I was overdoing my hospitality. Shirley was giving me an evil cold shoulder. I felt her dissatisfaction, but I just ignored it hoping it was just in my brain. I was a Manager at my job and Michelle looked up to me. I didn't throw my weight around at work, but Michelle had a level of respect for me as I came into the company with credentials and I was doing good things in management.

After small talk and snacks, Shirley and her henchman Kaarme did everything they could to openly belittle me during the Bible study. They did not even use one Scripture in the Bible study. This was one of the worst experiences I have had with someone from the outside being present. At one point, Michelle looked at me in shock as Shirley and Kaarme spoke negatively about me. She was probably wondering why I did not stand up for myself and why did I bring her to a place where these folks had no respect for me. At work, I didn't walk around depressed. I dressed well and carried myself with a high level of confidence because I was the best at what I did and I had a passion for my work. However, I did not bring that confidence to Bible study, and Michelle got to see me cower in silence.

Afterward, Kaarme even got Michelle's number to follow up with her to make sure the dirty job they did to discredit me was sealed. I decided at that point that I would never bring anybody to Bible study again, and I never did. This was a very depressing personal decision I made because all we talked about was spreading the Gospel to the world. But I was not convinced that my teachers believed I was part of that ministry. I was treated like I was somehow spiritually handicapped and they wanted to keep me that way.

After we lived together in Elizabeth and then in Newark, Shirley and her children moved into the Black House in another section of Newark. Shirley's kids, who were teenagers, did not have to cook or do any chores. The men in the Black House did not have to cook or clean either. The bathrooms were nasty and the females in The Group had to clean them. The first-floor bathroom was disgusting. The brothers' views of sexism and the degradation of women had trickled down from Daddy Leviathan's leadership as he gave the brothers full permission to see the sisters as slaves.

Ironically, all of the females in The Group (outside of Daddy Leviathan's inner crew of "wives") were the majority of money-makers, yet they found a way to bring us down. Kitchen duty with the sisters was another tortuous Shirley experience. Shirley was a great cook. However, all of the sisters in the house had to shop and prep all of the food. It was a Saturday night requirement that you prepped the food the night before, whether it was going to be a big breakfast or dinner. It would take the sisters and myself hours of cleaning and cutting collard greens, chicken, potatoes, and everything that went along with the meal. It was a lot of work, but Shirley and the brothers' demeanor were terrible towards us.

Shirley would spend the Bible study the day prior to kitchen duty, berating the women and speaking of how inadequate we were in the kitchen. The brothers, who did not have to lift a finger in the kitchen, mocked us and complained about how slow we worked. Shirley would top it off and say how we all had bad attitudes and the kitchen is the hotspot where attitudes fly. How were we supposed to be happy under a cold dictatorship? It was a vicious loop of religious slavery. If Shirley would have taken the time to teach us some of her cooking skills and all of us worked together as a team, the process would have been a lot better. It was literally a rigid dictatorship working for the queen to prep her food. All she had to do was come in and just add the ingredients together to cook for us all.

Shirley loved drama and liked to give examples of her point by showing a film. She showed us a comedy clip of Keystone Cops and compared us to the uncoordinated and idiotic men in the clip. She also compared us to the dodo birds in the *Ice Age* movie. She thrived on pointing out how idiotic all of us were, and everybody laughed and thought it was so funny. She had a way of making it seem as though her actions were more of a caring gesture than comedy or degradation. In my heart, I knew that she was being derogatory to all of us, and it wasn't funny to me at all.

I realize now that this was self-glorifying for her because she was praised as the high queen who was free from sin. She was an Elder, a chosen one in the open-door prophets who would teach the world. However, everything Shirley did demonstrated her lack of leadership and insecurity. If we were really the church of the open door and the School of the Prophets, there would have been growth after over 20 years of teaching the same group of people. How could we all still be idiotic? Doesn't she know this is a direct reflection of her leadership?

*"Before you are a leader, success is all about growing yourself. When you become a leader, success is all about growing others. "*
### Jack Welch

In essence, The Group was involved in idol worship. We had been around for decades and in fact, we were like The Keystone Cops because we could not work together, we did not trust each other, we argued constantly, and there were constant struggles as comrades for Christ. We were programmed to only trust the Elders as they were all-knowing and walked with God. No matter how much studying of the Bible we completed, we would *never* be anything more than what the Elders deemed us—servants and second-class human beings.

As I stated, when I came into The Group, my hopes, dreams, and aspirations were to take the gospel of Jesus Christ to the world. I wanted to learn the Scriptures and be a teacher or preacher by using whatever gifts God has given me. The more I took care of Shirley and her family, the less I was regarded. Shirley told me after decades in The Group that Daddy Leviathan told her that as far as he's concerned about me, "This is as good as she is ever going to get. Basically, all she can do is be a financial provider because she doesn't have any other gifts. There is nothing for her to work on. She just needs to be glad to watch the action." All of the Elders treated many of us as second-class citizens. They often reminded us not to have aspirations, but to be honored to be part of a growing congregation to support "Daddy's vision."

After being ridiculed, hurt, embarrassed, and torn down for over two decades in The Group, I just learned how to be silent. By keeping my mouth shut, I accepted my place and acted like a bumbling idiot anytime I was around Shirley so that she would be okay. If I displayed any kind of wisdom, I was a threat to her, the queen. *All hail to the Queen Mother*!

## Idol Worship

During nearly every "Bible Study" class, Shirley spoke praises of Daddy Leviathan. She made sure to keep our idolatry of him very fresh by speaking of the innumerable great works that he has done. One night she spoke of being in a store with him and his concubine gang and he told her to go to the back of the store and look at the shelf. She always boasted how obedient she was to his every word. She stated when she went to the back, there were porn tapes on the shelf. We all laughed because it was portrayed that he was just messing with her to see her response.

Now fast forward to a year after I left, I was told by Doc who left The Group that Daddy Leviathan and his concubine gang watched porn together. I believed what she said because at that time I saw them watching a new HBO show that was released called "Real Sex." What man of God watches porn or sexually explicit shows with other female members of the congregation besides his own wife? Doc also told me there was an epidemic of venereal diseases among the women.

Shirley made it her life's work to make sure we knew what our place was with respect to Leviathan. During a Bible Study, she raised her head and blurted out with pride like she was a great poet, "He is the Sun and we are the planets that revolve around him!" When she said that, everyone threw their hands up in shouts of praise like this was the most profound thing that was ever said.

We became so programmed that those of us who remained in the U.S., operated in idol worship even when Shirley would spend months in Ghana with Daddy Leviathan and his wives. Regardless of who was teaching Bible Study, we would always start class with testimonies to speak great things, not about each other, but of the Elders Shirley and Daddy Leviathan. We completely missed the experience of brotherly love. We missed seeing and cultivating the good in each other. We did not have strong interpersonal relationships because the Elders made sure we were loyal to them and not each other. I dare someone to tell me this is *not* idol worship.

# CHAPTER 17

# THE ELITE AND IMPS

*"Bad people don't go to hell, they are already there."*
**Dan Millman**

The students from Montclair University who had been with The Group since its inception were members of the Elite Class. Other members of the Elite class included Daddy's Leviathan's legal wife, her sister, and other family members.

## Elder Lela, The Forgotten Wife

Lela is Leviathan's first and only legal wife. She has become the greatest victim of us all. She stayed with him and is still supporting him, his wives, and their children. How can a woman accept the fact that her husband not only has sex with women of the congregation, but he also traveled with them and then lived with them, away from her and his children? This was subtly being done in the open before us all, but we were blinded to it because it was under the guise of these women being Daddy Leviathan's student disciples.

As I mentioned, he openly transitioned into living with his female Montclair University students in the basement of his home, with his wife and five children living upstairs. He had a bedroom in the basement and had private visitors with a private entrance. He established what was called an Elite team of students that were likened to disciples. These women (and one brother who left after a year) were considered to be at heightened levels of spirituality. Leviathan met with this team privately from the rest of the congregation. They were the envy of all of us who were not part of the Elite Team. I and others dreamed of being selected one day.

There was one of us, Michelle, who was actually initiated into this team. Michelle was a beautiful sister with caramel skin, long curly locks, and big brown eyes—a Rhianna look-alike. She had a heart of gold and was so pleasant to be around. She could preach, teach, exhort, and encourage the congregation with so much grace. This was the sister that was later to be found caught having sex with Leviathan by her husband. One of her three children is suspected to be Leviathan's and not her husband's.

This team of beautiful Elites was a cloak for him to privately be with his harem and entertain in sexual orgies during his "private classes with the Elite Team." For years he lived in the basement while Lela was raising the small children on the first floor of their Elizabeth home. In those years while I lived in that house with his wife and children, twice Daddy Leviathan came upstairs to have sex with me when no one was around. Those were the years when my sanity began to slip, and long-term sickness was around the corner.

Lela and Leviathan's firstborn son went through a hellish time as he entered puberty and found out about his father's infidelity. To The Group, he was portrayed as a rebellious, stubborn child who was always getting a big whipping from his father. As he entered his teenage years, he knew exactly what was happening and it disturbed him. Eventually, he left the house at an early age. I wonder if Lela knows deep in her heart that she and Leviathan are to blame for their child's pain.

As a few years went on, someone rented a home for Leviathan and his family in Irvington, New Jersey. This was the transition from integrating his wife and children to living with about seven young women in their early 20s. He and his wife were in their 30s. Instead of living in the basement, he lived on the top floor loft with a few of the women that "took care of him" like ironing his clothes, combing his hair, and running errands, including Shirley. He was treated as a king.

Although Lela knew what was going on, she respected him and honored him as the prophet of God. Lela is revered as an Elder and is known for her powerful prayer and singing voice. She and her twin sister Lulu had gifts of singing and heartfelt, fiery preaching. They inherited these gifts from their mother, Ma Shoemaker. I still believe Lela is the greatest victim and I pray that as she reads this book, her eyes will be enlightened to know she supported a sick, perverted man.

## Elder Lulu
### Robbing Peter and Taking From Paul

Lulu, the twin sister of Lela, was Daddy Leviathan's armor bearer. In the Old Testament, an armor bearer is selected by the king or general for their bravery, and they protect the king at all times. In the church, armor bearers assist the pastor in whatever he or she needs to be done. I guess you can equate Lulu's bravery to the fact that she would not back down from anyone and be persistent in getting what she wanted. I have witnessed her charismatic and ruthless bargaining and negotiation skills. She used her favor and weight as an Elder to get us to cash in our 401Ks and give, give, give. Lulu was the main person behind Shirley that shuffled the big funds arriving from the U.S. by those who worked. She made sure that Leviathan and his women had wine, weed, beer, and plenty of food while the rest of the folks at Bronibyma, including the Ghanains that lived with them, ate last, or had little to eat.

In the early days, I had much love and respect for Lulu. I learned how to sing from her and Lela. They portrayed women of great humility and women who not only loved God but loved everyone. But as time progressed, she showed her true alliance to Daddy Leviathan and her marriage paid the price. She left her husband and children to move to Ghana with Daddy Leviathan in 1998.

A few years prior to her departure, her eldest daughter got pregnant. As I looked at the situation, I saw that her daughter Esther was ostracized because of it and she left her family in shame. I believe this was one of Lulu's biggest failures.

A number of years after I left The Group, Lulu's son Mickey died. She didn't even send money to the family to help out with the funeral, nor did she show up in time. Lulu was literally a day late and a dollar short when she showed up from Ghana. During this time, I had a good relationship with her daughter Esther, who did my hair. I felt so bad for Esther and the rest of the family so I helped pay for the funeral.

Lulu's second failure was that she was so wrapped up serving Daddy Leviathan. Lulu burned so many bridges at food stores in Ghana, taking food on credit, not paying it back, and then moving to the next store to be victimized by her. She turned into a person that lacked integrity, a thief, and the biggest idol worshiper of Daddy Leviathan. If Daddy Leviathan wanted something, she would burn down a bridge to get it.

## If It Acts Like a Snake

The manner in which the brothers and leaders of The Group treated women was shameful. There was one sub-leader who epitomized evil. I will call him Kaarme because it means snake. Although he was not in the Elite class, he was one class below, which was the Salvation class. Kaarme was the highest ranked in the Salvation class, and he was the wickedest, most evil person I have ever encountered.

Kaarme is the closest human being to emulate my concept of Satan. He had a dynamic gift of preaching and teaching. Kaarme was sharp and skillful with the word, but he did not have an ounce of love in his heart. I consider Kaarme a reflection of Daddy Leviathan—Daddy Leviathan liked young girls and women, and Kaarme liked young boys and men. Kaarme was Shirley's right hand man. The two of them were the biggest gossipers and mean-spirited leaders in The Group. Kaarme would openly say the most wicked things to other commoners or me, and he was rarely if ever, chastised. The Elders gave him the green light to tear us down at will. I believe Kaarme was off-limits to be spoken to because he knew all the dirty secrets of Daddy Leviathan and Elite leaders.

As I stated, there was so much backbiting amongst the "saints." Although he was Shirley's right-hand henchman, privately, she told the sisters that she did not trust him. Yet in Bible study, there was constant brown-nosing of each other. They were always laughing and belittling everyone and portrayed that they had a tight relationship. For years, I was the butt of many inside jokes between the two of them. Kaarme and Shirley had the same flow during Bible study, especially when they were hurling accusations at someone. They played off each other well, but at the end of the day, their relationship was fake.

Kaarme hated me from the beginning because he knew that I was on the outside of Daddy Leviathan's harem. My low status made me prime meat for him to look down upon—like I was trash. Kaarme was the head of the brothers' house in Elizabeth. There were other communal houses in Elizabeth as well. The brother's house was always dirty, and the bathroom was disgusting. At one point for a few months, there was a dead rat in the house so the smell was unbearable. We had a few Bible studies at the house, and I was relieved there weren't many more.

I never understood how they emphasized that the leaders were free from sin, yet Kaarme would be chosen to preach out of all of us at other churches, and he was having affairs with multiple single and married men. So many of the married brothers were having sex with the sisters. I guess since Daddy Leviathan was leading the way, there was nothing anyone could say about it, so others followed suit.

Early on, Shirley named me Adora, a warrior princess of power. I was proud of the name because I was strong and athletic, so the name fit me well. However, Kaarme decided he would start a pitbull breeding business to make money. He got his first female pitbull, who bled all over the house, and he named her Adora. Initially, I wasn't aware of the dog's name. One night at Bible study, Kaarme kept calling out "Adora, Adora" in a sly manner. Every time he said it, he was laughing. I didn't realize it was his pitbull's name until afterward. I was upset that Shirley did not even talk to him and tell him to change the dog's name. It was disrespectful to have a woman in the congregation with the same name as a dog. My pseudo-name stuck with me until I left The Group.

Kaarme was a criminal. He would use the Social Security numbers of people in the congregation who did not work. He claimed them as dependents on his income taxes to get a higher refund. He stole the identities of the brothers and opened credit cards, and took out loans in their names. He used one of the brother's identities to buy a car and destroyed his credit because he didn't pay the monthly loan payments. No matter how much wrongdoing or evil Kaarme did, none of the Elders spoke to him, chastised him, or took away his power.

At one point, Kaarme left The Group and I was so happy! One less leader tearing me down. However, unfortunately, he came back after a few years. I guess he couldn't make it in the real world because no one would take his crap. He had to be amongst his cruel co-conspirators to make him feel important. I was so annoyed when he returned, and Shirley chastised us because we didn't welcome him with open arms. There was nothing new about him—no humility, no love. Kaarme came back with a worse attitude than when he left. He was still a rude, gossiping loudmouth, telling people off every chance he got.

Maybe Kaarme continued to harass me because he wanted Amaro, my crush. Amaro confided in me that Kaarme had been hitting on him. Amaro preferred women. Kaarme knew that Amaro was interested in me. One day I called the house to speak to Amaro while we were courting and Kaarme hung up on me. Years after I left The Group, Amaro told me he was one of the identities that Kaarme stole.

Like Daddy Leviathan, when Kaarme set his sights on a man, he was going to get him. Kaarme had gotten a new job and worked with a man named James, a tall, handsome, married former football player. James got saved through Kaarme, and Kaarme baptized him. We all went to the baptism. James's wife was a beautiful professional model. James came to Bible study from New York City every night in his wife's red Mazda 626. He drove that car into the ground. He had already begun to show signs of recklessness that was rampant throughout the congregation. As time progressed, James fell into Kaarme's lair and they began a sexual relationship that continues to this day.

Shirley gave me and a few other sisters the inside scoop on James and Kaarme. James's wife found out what was going on. She recorded a lover's conversation between James and Kaarme and confronted him. His wife called Shirley to tell her what was going on and to help save her marriage. Shirley wanted a badge of honor and claimed she tried her best to save James's marriage by taking both of them out to *Sylvia's* in Harlem. But James chose to continue in his behavior and his wife filed for divorce. James swiftly moved into the house where I and a few sisters lived down the street from the Black House.

Kaarme and James moved in downstairs with me and three other sisters. That was when I caught them red-handed taking a shower together. Then I went to Shirley because the Scripture says to bring things to the Elders if there are discrepancies or disagreements that could not be resolved amongst each other. I also thought to myself, *now I really have something on them. There is no way that this act can be defended by the Elders."* When I told Shirley she told me to ask them if this was a habit picked up in college or by another means. I was surprised that she did not say anything else about it. I followed her instructions and confronted them about taking the shower together, but they really did not respond or take me seriously. My report fizzled away.

One of the other sisters also told us one night James was acting weird and freaking out. He confessed to her that he did cocaine and he must have been in a really bad state before it wore down. James is now the face of the organization as CEO, allowing Leviathan to still be The Group's true leader while hiding behind James' title . The Group stopped publicly stating they are a ministry and now touts being a nonprofit organization providing online education to students abroad.

It was almost deranged the way Kaarme always attacked me. For years he would just shout at me, "You're crazy. You're crazy. Shut up." It was like he made a point to say something to me in public. The Group attended a lot of speak-easy clubs that featured open mic, poetry, spoken word, and music. One evening I was walking up to the stage to sing, and he kept making the cut-throat gesture for me not to go up. Even at my friend Darla's funeral, he approached me and called me names. He kept telling me to shut up and be quiet because I was crazy. Who talks to someone like that at a funeral? Again, no love, no compassion, and definitely no God.

I was called crazy for so many years that I started to believe it. However, it made no sense because I was very successful at work. I always thought if I was crazy, then where is their anointing to help me? Why are they not showing me love and mercy? Countless times there was no God in Kaarme's behavior. Instead, it was evil and satanic.

# CHAPTER 18

# GIVE GOOD MEASURE

*Give, and it shall be given unto you; good measure, pressed down, and shaken together, and running over, shall men give into your bosom. For with the same measure that ye mete withal it shall be measured to you again.*
**Luke 6:38 (KJV)**

The Group encouraged giving. They did not force it, but in Bible study, they were always talking about giving as a way to manipulate and etch into your mind and spirit as being one of the most important things you can do for The Group members overseas. They all relied on our giving. If someone gave their whole paycheck, they propped them up to be a symbol for others to do the same. I gave everything I had. More than 80% of my earnings were given straight from my heart. I wanted to be accepted. I wanted to help the less fortunate overseas and I wanted to be beloved by the Elders and the people. Most of all I wanted to please God.

If there's one good thing they can say about me is that I was a giver. Giving connected with me as I believe it is innate to who I am. When I left The Group, I had zero dollars in my bank savings account even though I was making six figures. Shirley made a point to keep saying to us, "When you give to The Group, it is none of your business what the money will be used for!" I never asked for accountability, and I don't believe I would have gotten it anyway. You were frowned upon if you did not give all of your tax returns and show from paycheck to paycheck your support of the "ministry in Ghana."

I was so trusting of Shirley and my best friend Dolores who handled all of The Group's financial transactions and taxes, that I added Dolores to my bank account so that she could freely make withdrawals as needed. The only reporting of taxes done under their 501(c)3 is based on checks received from the members with a cap on the dollar amount of donations we report on our tax filings to the IRS. Any cash given to The Group did not get reported. I know this because I pushed back one year when Dolores prepared my taxes. In 2010 she only allowed me to report a $36,000 donation to The Group on my taxes because she would have to report it under The Group's taxes. The Group received far more than this amount from me that year. As an example, below is Image #1 that shows in 2010, I gave a total of $11,000 in checks provided to the organization between February 17th and March 1st.

## Image #1

Image #2 below shows a $9000 personal check written and other cash withdrawals to donate during the months of March and April 2010 that were sent by Western Union to The Group.

## Image #2

**CHASE** ⬡

March 13, 2010 through April 14, 2010
Primary Account: ███████████

### CHECKS PAID

| CHECK NO. | DESCRIPTION | DATE PAID | AMOUNT |
|-----------|-------------|-----------|--------|
| 530  ^ | | 04/08 | $9,000.00 |
| **Total Checks Paid** | | | **$9,000.00** |

If you see a description in the Checks Paid section, it means that we received only electronic information about the check, not the original or an image of the check. As a result, we're not able to return the check to you or show you an image.

^ An image of this check may be available for you to view on Chase.com.

### ATM & DEBIT CARD WITHDRAWALS

| DATE | DESCRIPTION | | AMOUNT |
|------|-------------|--|--------|
| 03/15 | Card Purchase | 03/13 Delta Air  00623232 Los Angeles CA Card 4789 | $1,610.70 |
| 03/15 | ATM Withdrawal | 03/14 10 Franklin Street Bloomfield NJ Card 8219 | 500.00 |
| 03/15 | ATM Withdrawal | 03/14 10 Franklin Street Bloomfield NJ Card 8219 | 400.00 |
| 03/15 | ATM Withdrawal | 03/14 1000 Railroad Ave Woodmere NY Card 4789 | 200.00 |
| 03/15 | ATM Withdrawal | 03/12 181 Franklin Street Bloomfield NJ Card 8219 | 120.00 |
| 03/15 | ATM Withdrawal | 03/14 1000 Railroad Ave Woodmere NY Card 4789 | 100.00 |

Total amount of cash I donated from these images which only represent three months of the year already totaled $20,000. These funds are outside of the monthly $2,500 donations given to The Group which is $30,000 annually. These three months of giving are the biggest out of the entire year because, annually The Group spends thousands of dollars preparing for Daddy Leviathan's birthday in May.

I began to write checks in my last years of being with The Group because I saw that cash as a waste of money. I was unaware that this was also an illegal practice. I wrote as many checks as I could, but Dolores would make withdrawals because they always needed cash sent to them almost every other day. Many of us got temporary blocks from Western Union because money was being sent so frequently, they suspected fraud. Dolores would use almost every member of the congregation's name to send money to Ghana to throw Western Union off. As deceitful liars, The Group underreported their tax donations from me and all of the other members. Then to ensure they took every penny we had to our name, The Elders used their fear tactics to get us to donate whatever tax refunds we got. It was all perfect timing to prepare for Daddy Leviathan's annual birthday bash so that we could lavish him with gold, clothes, and food from the U.S. or have folks like me travel that time of the year to sacrifice a suitcase to bring the frozen goods and meats for the celebration.

Dolores was a big giver like myself. She was well-educated and intelligent. Her desire was always to serve and give. She always had the baddest cars in the congregation. At one point she had a black Firebird and then moved on to get a beautiful black SUV. After that, she stuck with SUVs. Dolores was a road warrior and one of the best drivers I knew. She was also one of the dearest friends I had. The friendship did fall short when I was put on the spot after I got her a job reporting to me.

Dolores complained to Shirley about me not getting up in time to ride to work with her. That was the only hurtful thing I can remember about our relationship, but I forgave her because the system was set up for us to "tattle tale" on each other and not confide in one another. Granted, we were adults in our 30s, but "Bible Study" classes were spent much of the time openly chastising folks like me who could not do anything right. Nevertheless, during a rare time, Dolores confided in me that Daddy Leviathan and his imps drove one of her cars on multiple occasions and ran up several parking tickets. Instead of apologizing and finding out how they could help pay, they just chucked the tickets to the side, leaving her to pay for them.

Another member bought Daddy Leviathan a van. He ended up going bankrupt due to so many other sacrifices that he made for The Group. I'm not sure if he knew that the van he bought for Daddy Leviathan was used for orgies, weed-smoking, and beer-drinking with all of the women that he drove around with. There was rarely if ever a brother in the van with Daddy Leviathan and his concubine tribe of women.

Years later, I learned from a former member who worked at a hospital and found medical records that Birdie had an abortion during her time in The Group which caused a number of folks to fall away. They all assumed it was Daddy Leviathan's seed and there were rumors of other women who had abortions prior to the move to Ghana. So Leviathan was having sexual relations with a mother and her daughter at the same time. Although victims themselves, all of these women still hold a great level of responsibility because they allowed their daughters to be prostituted by Daddy Leviathan and they helped enable his lifestyle. The same goes for Shirley, his number-one henchwoman. There were others, but I cannot even remember their names because some came and went.

Around 2010 one incident really pricked my spirit that provided insight into The Group's dynamics. As stated earlier, I was consistently giving over $2500/month to pay rent and give money towards the "ministry" for Daddy Leviathan and his wives in Ghana. This included one of his wives whom I bonded with as a friend when I visited. Mumu had a sincere love for me as a friend. We honored, respected each other, and sincerely enjoyed being friends. When Mumu was pregnant, I asked Daddy Leviathan's daughter Coco, who I was also close with, to ask her father if I could be the godmother. I wanted to help provide for the child. She quickly said that I was not worthy.

When I had that conversation with Coco I was driving. I had to pull over. I felt a knife go right through my heart and I couldn't breathe. I was a big financial supporter of her, as well. She quickly said she was joking, but I knew she wasn't. Even though we had grown to be close friends, there was still that dividing line. She was of "royal" seed and I was a commoner. I was sending her money each month faithfully for years not to buy friendship, but to support her in the ministry she was doing. I never asked where the money went. I just gave because I trusted her heart. But that comment brought a quick reality check of the culture that was created and I knew that I would never fit in. There was nothing I could ever do to make it into the "in-crowd."

Although my heart hurt and I spent years yearning, burning inside, and crying to be accepted, I thank God that my request was never granted. If so, I would have been living a lie because I would have idolized a man instead of honoring the true and living God. How can I serve a man who dishonored his marriage and so many other people's marriages with his selfish acts of lust, pedophilia, and adultery? How can I love someone like that more than God? That is blasphemous, but that was the path that I tried to pursue and I thank God I failed!

Later Daddy Leviathan granted me to be the godmother, but it never felt right. He was reluctant to give me that title. I just wanted to show kindness to his wife because she was so kind to me. I never pursued or became that child's godmother. The damage done was quite deep.

*"Without resources, nothing can be achieved."*
**Marvin Winans**

I had a positive experience the year before I left The Group. Marvin Winans, the Grammy-winning singer from The Winans Gospel Family, met The Group during his travels to Ghana in the early to mid 2000s. Members of The Group made themselves known to him and he collaborated with us on a few events. In February of 2011, Kaarme and James contacted Marvin Winans and asked him to join The Group in a united distance learning event sponsored by Polygon and Vodafone. The event featured face-face communications between students in Ghana and the U.S.

This was before GoogleMeet and Zoom, so video conferencing was not common and required special equipment. This was a tactic that Kaarme and Shirley came up with to get funding and grants on behalf of The Group's 501(c) 3 status. They always spoke of seeking thousands of dollars in grants, but we never saw this on a large scale. Nevertheless, Marvin Winans accepted the invitation.

The First Lady of Ghana, Daddy Leviathan, and his entourage were attending on the Accra side while The Group's financial supporters and Marvin Winans attended on the U.S. side in Washington, DC at the Smithsonian National Museum of African Art.[3]

---

3    *https://www.ghanaweb.com/GhanaHomePage/NewsArchive/Meet-The-First-Lady-of-Ghana-and-Pastor-Marvin-Winans-203045*

Diasporia News of Sunday, 13 February 2011          Source:

## Meet The First Lady of Ghana and Pastor Marvin Winans

« Prev   Next »   Comments (2)   🎧 Listen to Article

-Transatlantic Celebration Press Release

Washington, DC and Accra, Ghana – On February 16, 2011 from 10am to 1pm,
and our corporate sponsors Polycom, Vodafone and the
United Distance Learning Association (UDLA) will host a celebration of
African and African American culture at the National Museum of African
Art/Smithsonian Institution in Washington, DC and the W.E.B. Du Bois
Memorial Centre for Pan-African Culture in Accra, Ghana. The event can be
viewed worldwide by a telecast made available through Polycom. The event
will feature live face to face interaction with participants from schools
from the US and Ghana. Discussions will be based on questions from
participants from both sides ranging in topics from everyday life, history
and culture. Each school will have 10 minutes to present their prepared
historical facts. The goal of the event is to celebrate our history and
culture on an international platform and introduce the program to officials
that can help implement the program throughout both countries.

"Each year          continues to advance its mission of sharing the rich
history and heritage of Africa through educational and cultural awareness to
all people." said          , CEO of          "We are
extremely excited about this year's event being held at two internationally
renowned venues. We will continue to have more of these collaborative events
not just for Black History Month, but all year long."

At the W.E.B. Du Bois Memorial Centre in Accra, it is our extreme honor and
privilege to have Her Excellency, First Lady of Ghana, Mrs. Ernestina Naadu
Mills as our guest speaker in Ghana. First Lady Mills is known for her
passion about young people and works hard to promote literacy, especially
for some of the girls in rural areas whose education is sometimes disrupted
by social pressures. In the US, we are excited to have welcoming remarks by
Dr. Johnnetta B. Cole because of her tireless efforts as an educator and
activist for social and economic justice. As our guest speaker, we have
Pastor Marvin L. Winans, the grammy-winning artist of the famed "Winans"
gospel group and chancellor of The Marvin L. Winans Academy of the
Performing Arts. We are pleased to have students from Howard
University, School Without Walls, New Hope Academy, E.L. Haynes Public
Charter School, Roosevelt High School and The Latin American Youth Center
attend the event live at the Smithsonian. Students from The Marvin L.Winans
Academy of the Performing Arts in Detroit, Tuskegee University in Tuskegee,
Alabama, Essex County College from Newark, NJ will participate via
telepresence. From Ghana, students from the Achimota School, University of
Accra, Kwame Nkrumah University of Science and Technology(KNUST) and Mate
Maise School from Cape Coast will participate in this celebratory event.

The Smithsonian National Museum of African Art, whose mission is to inspire

Kaarme and James were skilled con men. They could convince someone to sell their own mother. They talked up the event to Marvin Winans. His response was "I'll come when you send me a plane ticket." "Oh, of course, that was our intent," was their reply. Yet the God's honest truth was that they did not have any money. So during times like this, because of my great income, I was treated like a human being even though I knew they were faking it. They asked me to pay for Marvin Winan's ticket. They said they would pay me back, but I knew that was a lie. I conceded and paid for the ticket.

The time had finally arrived to greet Pastor Marvin Winans at the airport on the day of the event. Kaarme and James promised to take Marvin out for lunch. Of course, they came to me to pay for the lunch expenses. I was so honored and grateful to be in Marvin's presence and I was not going to just give money to take Mr. Winans out. I had to be present with them. The Winans' music is a part of my early days of salvation and my first experiences with God. When I was in college in Farmingdale, I remember feeling like there was something missing and sitting on my bed, crying. Then a funny commercial would come on the TV that would make me laugh. In some way, I felt God comforted me that night, even though I had not given my life to Him at that time. Then I heard their songs, "Straighten My Life Out Again," "When You Cry," and so many more heartfelt songs written and performed by The Winans. Their songs became a staple for the early days of being in The Group, providing comfort, strength, and happiness in my heart.

After we took Marvin to lunch, we headed back to the Smithsonian Museum to be in time for the cross-continental event using Polycom's donated telepresence equipment. At one point, Kaarme and James had to exit the SUV for a few moments and it was just me and Marvin Winans in the car. Marvin asked, "How does The Group fund these events and the initiatives that you all have?" I proudly gave him the answer that Shirley always says, "We do amazing things in Ghana with only a handful of workers in the U.S. This is a miracle of God that our small numbers can support so much." Whenever Shirley said this during Bible studies, the congregation always lifted their voice in high praise. "Thank You, God for the miracle!

Hallelujah," we would shout at the tops of our voices! I expected Marvin to respond in a favorable manner, but he didn't. Instead, he looked straight into my eyes. He turned his head sideways, looked up towards the sky, and said, "Without resources, nothing can be achieved. If we believe God is sending us on a path, at some point God has to send resources."

His words hit me between the eyes because we were victims of being stripped of all our resources to satisfy King Daddy Leviathan. One of the sisters who made a quarter of what I made always felt bad that she could not give as much as me or the other big money makers. But it didn't matter because we all lived together between two to three houses. Even with her meager salary, she was pressured by Lulu to cash in her 401K. She secretly expressed how this was an excessive act to require of us. These requests would come in from Lulu often to satisfy the lusts of Leviathan and his prized wives. The resources in the U.S. were being stripped, robbed, and raided. This was not God's way of supplying, especially since I saw how they were living during the times I visited Ghana.

I kept Marvin's words to myself. He was having a tough time understanding how The Group can last and grow with their current limited resources. I didn't have an answer for him. I wish I could personally thank Marvin Winans and tell him how much his words of wisdom are still impactful to me even years later as I pursue the new beautiful hopes and dreams that have been birthed in my heart. When Kaarme and James came back into the SUV, they took over as hosts of Marvin for the rest of the event. But I was grateful for those few moments that made me ponder in the months to come. Meeting Marvin Winans ended up being a bigger blessing than I planned. Little did I know that Pastor Winans planted a seed in me.

# Part III
# My Transition

*Pupa (Chrysalis): When the caterpillar is full grown and stops eating.*

*How long, Lord, must I cry for help?*
*But you do not listen!*
*I call out to you, "Violence!"*
*But you do not deliver!*
*Why do you force me to witness injustice?*
*Why do you put up with wrongdoing?*
*Habakkuk 1:3 (NET)*

# CHAPTER 19

# GHANA TRIP 2010

*After the LORD had spoken these words to Job, the LORD said to Eliphaz the Temanite: "My anger burns against you and against your two friends, for you have not spoken of me what is right, as my servant Job has.*
**Job 42:7 (ESV)**

My first surgery was in 2005 then five years later, in 2010 was sick again with anemia and a large belly full of new fibroid tumors. Yet my career was still on the rise as I was thriving and working hard. That year, I made plans to visit Ghana in the spring. Before the trip, I had a dream about Daddy Leviathan. In the dream, he looked like a giant Jabba the Hutt slug from Star Wars. The dream was dark and creepy and he was very derogatory towards me.

I nixed off the dream hoping for the best, but I did keep it in the memory banks of my mind. By the time I got back from my trip, I began to understand it because, again, he ignored me the entire time. I wanted to privately talk with him to get some understanding of what our relationship was about and discuss the "spiritual wife" thing again. Shirley's class about spiritual wives not getting touched by their husbands was spoken of openly. By this time, I had not been touched by him for 18 years, but the "spiritual wife" and no legal marriage didn't feel right to me. So, when I returned from that trip, I said in my heart, *I will give this one more year because I just can't take this anymore.*

At the end of that trip, the day before I left, Daddy Leviathan had me open up the Bible during Bible study. Daddy Leviathan had a habit of "opening up" the Bible randomly to see what message God specifically wants to say to you. I guess he expected me to open up to a random Scripture about doom and fear. I already had words written in my Bible during that trip that read, "If I don't trust Daddy, I am at risk of Blaspheming God" and "If I don't keep the blessing, doom awaits!" But I didn't have any of that in my mind because I really wanted to hear what God would say to me personally. I randomly opened up to Job 27 and my eyes fell on verse 3. I read up to verse 6 and I was blown away!

*" All the while my breath is in me, and the spirit of God is in my nostrils;*
*My lips shall not speak wickedness, nor my tongue utter deceit.*
*God forbid that I should justify you: till I die I will not remove mine*
*integrity from me.*
*My righteousness I hold fast, and will not let it go: my heart shall not*
*reproach me so long as I live."*

This Scripture definitely went over Daddy Leviathan's head and he didn't have a response after I read it. Nevertheless, after I came home, that summer was the most depressed I had felt in a long time because I felt so rejected and alone. I remember going to the drugstore and taking some over-the-counter drugs for depression which actually helped me. I took them for two months and I was able to prevent myself from losing my mind that summer.

When I returned home, I kept reading the Scripture over and over, especially "God forbid that I should justify you" which means that I don't need to accept the belittlement that Daddy Leviathan has pushed my way all these years. Job was putting the people he thought were his beloved friends in place. Job's friends condemned him and blamed him for his illness and misfortunes. Job finally spoke back in defense, putting his friends on notice that he has a pure soul and their condemning words were all lies.

The reading of this Scripture was a seed planted in me that aided in my eventual departure. It was only until years later that I truly understood the parallels of this which ties back to when I taught Bible Study at Farmingdale. I taught a series on the book of Job until another student, a relative of the famous gospel singer that was popular at that time, busted up the Bible Studies. He felt he should be leading the classes instead. He was a big tall light skinned guy who acted like he had more authority and bullied me out of leading the classes.

## GHANA TRIP 2011

In April 2012, Darla and I both had surgeries. Hers was a total hysterectomy with the hope to remove ovarian cancer. Unfortunately, as the year progressed, the cancer spread to the rest of her body. Six months prior to my surgery, I made my last visit to Ghana. The dream I had where Leviathan was like a giant Jabba the Hut slug still resonated with me and in my heart. I had distanced myself from Daddy Leviathan. I purposed in myself that when I go this time, I'm not going to try to be in Daddy Leviathan's space. I'm not going to ask him any questions. I was just going to go and have a good time and enjoy the friends I had over there. I developed beautiful relationships with some of the people.

It was clear that I was being used, but I was struggling with being obedient to Daddy Leviathan. I had a renewed sense of confidence and strength. It was the first time I went to Ghana and I purposely did not give Daddy Leviathan the time of day. My purpose was not to see him at all. I needed to prove to myself that I didn't want or need him anymore. I spent time at the school teaching the kids science. I traveled around Ghana enjoying the sites and sounds with others from The Group. It was wonderful. Daddy Leviathan wasn't on my mind.

I became sick during the trip and was lucky if I got two meals a day. It was so clear to me that the treatment of belittlement was Daddy Leviathan's caste culture at work, especially with the local Ghanaian children and young adults that lived with him. I saw how most of the things we bought in the U.S. for the Ghanains were for his family to receive the first fruits, leaving whatever was left for the "second class" Ghanaian citizens. So much for being a leader of a ministry of giving!

I saw how they prepared wonderful meals for him and his wives while the Ghanaian children were hungry. After I returned from the trip, I purchased a beautiful artist set for one of the Ghanaian children that I saw loved to do artwork. The child never received it. Instead, it was given to one of Daddy Leviathan's children. The reverse also happened to me. A custom dress was made made for me by

Coco as a gift, but as Shirley was about to hand it to me, she looked at it and took it for herself instead.

One thing that I always had going for me was my ability to connect with young children. I knew how to make them laugh, I loved teaching them science, songs and doing fun things. When I met the youngest of Daddy Leviathan's daughters, she was about five or six years old. She was already programmed to be one who is privileged and she was so mean and nasty to me when we first met, pointing her finger in my face and speaking insults and it hurt me very much. How can a small child be so evil? Then I realized she learned all of this from her mother and father. This helped me to turn my attention to giving my love and attention to the Ghanaian children who welcomed me with open arms because it was clear that I could not really connect with any of his children that were born in Ghana.

Nevertheless, during this trip, I completely ignored Daddy Leviathan and I felt I had arrived! I was finally finding happiness and strength in being who I am even though I still felt very inferior because of the caste system he created. The greatest part of that trip was the last 10 minutes at the house. Me and other members were planning to leave for the airport and we were all in one house gathering our things. Daddy Leviathan was alone in a room with one of the 17-year-old sisters, Selma, whom he impregnated and hid it from her parents. See the Afro-American Family In Ghana chart below.

# Afro-American Family in Ghana

This is a family of sisters with American and Ghanaian roots whose parents handed them over to The Group in Ghana to be educated. They lived at the house campus in Bronybima, where Daddy Leviathan and his wives lived. This campus has Daddy Leviathan's clan and a lot of children (young boys and girls) that were part of the school. This family of girls were molested and taken in as Daddy Leviathan's women. Selma's pregnancy was hidden when the children's father became concerned about his daughters' well-being.

## Etta

The eldest daughter has children by Leviathan when she was in her late teen/early 20's

## Olivia

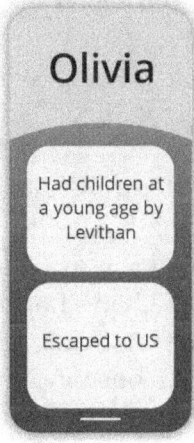

Had children at a young age by Levithan

Escaped to US

## Selma

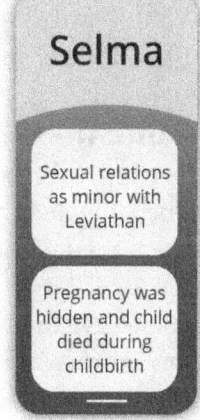

Sexual relations as minor with Leviathan

Pregnancy was hidden and child died during childbirth

## Amanda

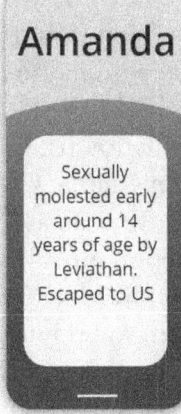

Sexually molested early around 14 years of age by Leviathan. Escaped to US

## Jade

Unsure if anything happened

He approached me quietly and then brought me into the bathroom. He tried to embrace me and put his hands on me. The great thing was that it was almost like there was an invisible shield around my body. It was as if he was trying to pat me, but stopped without touching me. I just stood there with no desire towards him and no fear. At that point, I knew I had won. I knew I did what I set out to accomplish. I needed to experience the feeling of not wanting or needing him and it was incredible!

When I got on that plane I knew I was free from him. I was so happy that he could not even touch me. I must have known deep down this was the beginning of my exit. I felt a freedom in my spirit that I had never felt before.

## THE GREAT I AM

My second fibroid removal surgery was performed by a well-renowned Black surgeon who, thankfully, prevented a hysterectomy and removed 48 fibroid tumors in April 2012.

I was still living in Elizabeth in a house full of sisters, but in order for me to get the proper help and care, I recovered from this second major surgery at the Black House in Newark. Unlike the chaos of the first surgery, there was a sister that took care of me with love and care and did a beautiful job. My friend Dolores also gave up her room for me because it was right across the hall from the sister that was helping me. But Dolores's room was also right next to Shirley's big room. Shirley had the nicest, biggest room in the Black House.

I was unable to walk downstairs for the first two weeks so I missed the Bible studies that she taught downstairs in the living room. Shirley had recently returned from Ghana, so everyone gathered to hear the stories she told about her trip. So as I'm healing, I'm listening to this really beautiful instrumental music by a harp player named Andreas Vollenweider. I used to have his albums in college and remembered how much I loved them, so I downloaded a few of my favorite albums. His music put me in a great mindful space of peace and healing. One day as I was meditating while listening to the music, I heard something deep down in my soul that I will never ever forget: *I Am Greater than The Group*. I was like wow! These words just slipped right into my soul with so much ease and they brought the greatest sense of peace. The Great I AM spoke to my heart to enlighten me that He is Greater than anyone else on this Earth. It initiated a loosening of The Group's hooks in my mind and soul.

There was one final incident that sealed the deal. Everyone knew I'm a big Tom Cruise movie lover. *Mission Impossible* came out. Shirley had the big TV and surround system in her bedroom and there were times me and a few sisters would watch movies with her. Since I was in the room next door to her and she had just returned from Ghana, I wanted to spend a little time with her, especially since I was unable to go downstairs for Bible studies.

I asked, "Hey Shirley, can we watch *Mission Impossible: Ghost Protocol* together?" She previously mentioned she had the DVD. Her response was "I don't care." I never really caught it or believed she meant it when she would express herself like that to me. Looking back she would often say the same words if I asked to join her when she went shopping or to spend time with her and the sisters when we gathered in her room. A week later I asked her a second time and I got no response so I just left it alone. I got the message she didn't want to hang with me and I was ok with that. So, two weeks passed by and I'm now able to go downstairs to Bible study again. Just like with my first surgery, I'm all excited to finally be able to attend. Lo and behold, Shirley begins to complain about me right in the middle of the study. She said I was very inconsiderate because I asked her to watch the movie. How dare I ask her when she watched it many times while she was in Ghana?

Everyone in the room began chastising me and sending me negative energy "How dare you do this to the Queen!" That was it for me. I went back to the room. As I lay on my bed, I knew it was wrong. Something snapped in me. For the first time, in my heart, I called it for what it was. I didn't say anything and I didn't apologize. Any kind of connection and love that I had for her, she disconnected it right then and there. It was like she cut the umbilical cord herself and I didn't even have to do it. I didn't have to fight back nor did I have to reason with her. She could have told me when I asked the first time, "Girl I am so tired of watching that movie. Maybe you can watch it with some of the other sisters." But no, she chose to openly embarrass me and openly use her authority to belittle me and have everyone else join in.

After that, I was having phone conversations with Leviathan's daughter Coco, located in Ghana, who confided in me how mean Shirley was towards her and how she felt trapped. When Shirley goes to live in Ghana for part of the year, Coco is the one cleaning her room and bathroom. I was so grateful that Coco opened up to me because I felt Shirley's meanness and coldness for years but was unable to say anything. I was able to freely tell Coco what happened with Shirley and after hearing her story, it gave me peace knowing that my judgment of Shirley was accurate all along. I was finally able to go back to the house where the sisters lived in Elizabeth and continued to heal quietly.

## SUMMER OF 2012

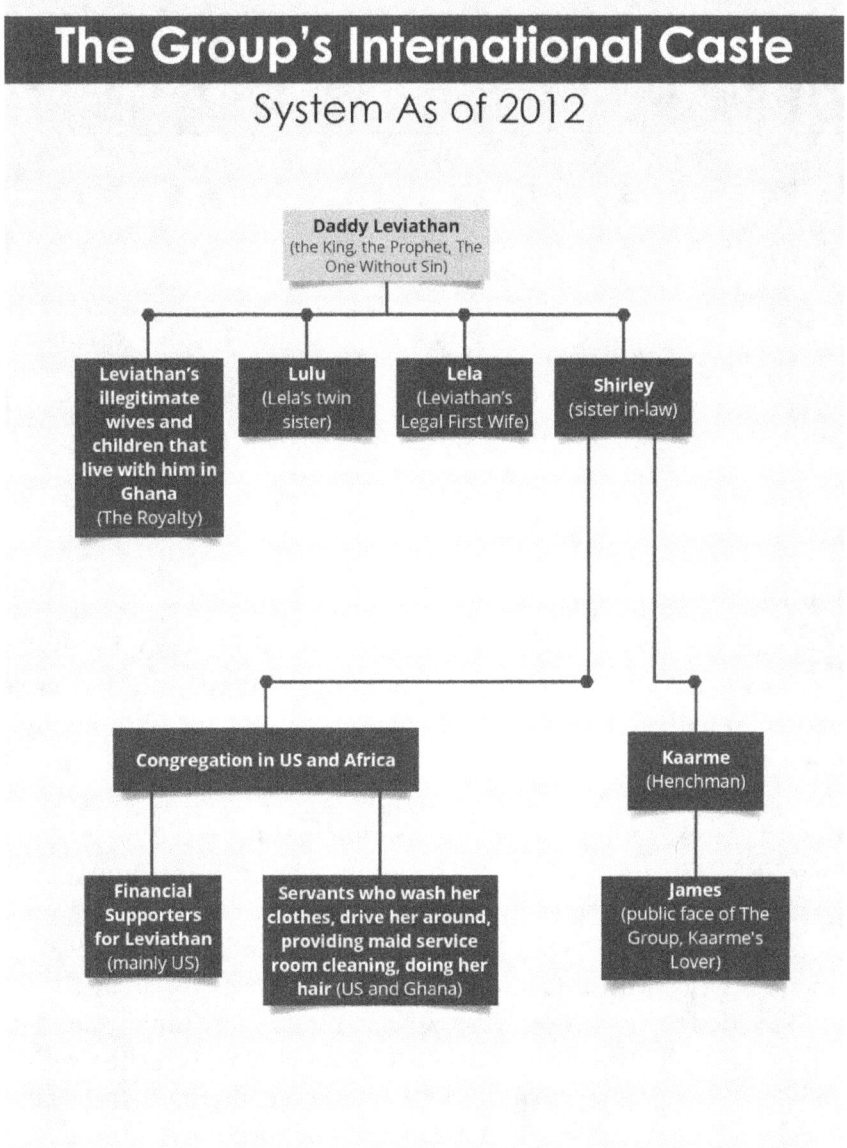

**The Group's International Caste**
System As of 2012

**Daddy Leviathan**
(the King, the Prophet, The One Without Sin)

**Leviathan's illegitimate wives and children that live with him in Ghana** (The Royalty)

**Lulu** (Lela's twin sister)

**Lela** (Leviathan's Legal First Wife)

**Shirley** (sister in-law)

**Congregation in US and Africa**

**Kaarme** (Henchman)

**Financial Supporters for Leviathan** (mainly US)

**Servants who wash her clothes, drive her around, providing maid service room cleaning, doing her hair** (US and Ghana)

**James** (public face of The Group, Kaarme's Lover)

# CHAPTER 20

# A NEW ATTITUDE

*"I'm feeling good from my hat to my shoe*
*Know where I am going and I know what to do*
*I've tidied up my point of view*
*I've got a new attitude..."*
**Patti Labelle**

A few months after my surgery, I went on a mission to lose weight. I was looking good and feeling great about myself. I started to pray on my own, building a newer and deeper relationship with God. I had lost 20 pounds by August 2012. I bought a beautiful white casual dress and wore it to Bible study. I was testifying and expounding on the Scriptures and Kaarmi interrupted me and started telling me off right in the middle of the Bible study. He said, "Who are you talking to and why are you looking at me?" I wasn't thinking about him at all. I was happy. I was feeling good about myself and my life in God. The words in the Scriptures must have stung his heart unbeknownst to me so he went on a rant.

I decided after all these years of being bullied by him to stand up to him. Finally, I had no fear because I saw him for who he was, despite the fact knowing that Shirley would come to his defense since this news would get back to her. I was already feeling detached from The Group because I had recently had a phone conversation with Daddy Leviathan asking him to release me. I told him I didn't want to be one of these "spiritual wives." His response let me know that all of my fears of being used and abused were true. He said, "Well I never stopped you from getting married to whoever you wanted to be married to." This confirmed I never had a relationship with him and that the "spiritual wife" scenario was a lie and he just ran through me like any low-class user and abuser on the street would do.

The holy veil of this man in my mind was shed and God revealed the true Daddy Leviathan. So for the first time, I openly spoke back to Kaarme during that Bible study and a big hush fell over the room. Then all hell broke loose and he got up right in my face. Dr. Sherry, one of Daddy Leviathan's wives was visiting from Ghana and since she positioned herself in authority above all of us as a wife of Daddy Leviathan, she commanded me to be quiet and just shut up. I told her I'm not afraid of him and that what he just did was wrong.

The sisters rushed me upstairs and Sherry started opening up the Bible like Daddy Leviathan always does and she picked out Scriptures on being quiet. She said, "Look, you're wearing a white dress and you don't want your soul to get stained by the situation." But to me, I was just telling the truth. Then I dropped the bomb on all of the sisters. I told them that Daddy Leviathan used me sexually. At that point, one of the sisters took me to another room and we prayed together. It was such a powerful and awesome prayer, and I felt something break in me spiritually. It was like a stronghold was loosed and I was freed.

Word got out what I said about Daddy Leviathan and Shirley called me a few days later. She asked me what happened and I told her the truth. I was expounding on a Scripture and Kaarme verbally attacked me, using Bible study to vent whatever hate he had towards me. Shirley immediately cut me off and lit into me that I needed to see how wrong I was. I let her say whatever she needed to say, but it was clear to me how off she was. It was such a ridiculous game of her knowing how evil this man is. My mind went back to the memory when after a hell night, Daddy Leviathan himself told me that Shirley does not have good judgment. She must have gotten wind of his sayings at that time. So, she deceived some of us and said to a select few of the sisters, "Daddy Leviathan is telling his wives I lack judgment, but he is just testing them to see how they will treat me."

But on this day, those memories came back to me along with re-cent events and all the years of how she treated me. The last ounce of respect I had for her was finally put out by her own words and ac-tions. What Kaarme did to me was seen and heard by everyone. Shir-ley could have asked anyone that was in the room and they would not have told her anything different. My regard for Shirley was total-ly diminished from that day forward.

# CHAPTER 21

# MY FOREVER SISTER

*"A sister can be seen as someone who is both ourselves and very much not ourselves - a special kind of double."*
**Toni Morrison**

The sisters of The Group were the real breadwinners. We provided for the Elders financially in every aspect of their lives. Again, I took care of Shirley's family, and Darla, a systems engineer, brought Lulu and her children a house and took care of them. Dolores, a Software Tester, bought the infamous Black House for Daddy Leviathan. Of all the sisters that came and left The Group, there was something about Darla that always connected with me.

We finished college around the same time and she was also an engineer with a Master degree in Electrical Engineering from the prestigious University of California in Berkeley. Darla bought a house in Elizabeth which ended up being a "house of women." The house also had two brothers that lived on the first floor. Darla lived on the third floor. During my last seven years in The Group, I lived with Darla at the house of women. Both Darla and I suffered from uterine fibroids which is common in African American women and may affect their fertility. My mom and sister had uterine fibroids, yet they each had five kids.

Since Darla and I were going through the same health issues which were discovered in the mid to late 1990s, we were both trying to take a healthy route and change our diet and went to nutritionists.

Darla was strict with her diet. She was eating tofu, juicing every-thing, and reduced her meat intake. I was not that strict, but I did make some notable adjustments that are with me to this day. We were both hard workers but at one point she became hermit-like and never left the house, working from home.

At the beginning of 2012, Darla started having a lot of pain and by this time she looked like she was seven or eight months pregnant and very pale. Darla was diagnosed with cancer. She went in to have surgery to remove the cancer, but it had already spread throughout her body. I was still healing from my surgery and was in the midst of my six weeks of recovery. Darla came home and she lost a lot of weight. She was undergoing chemotherapy. It was sad to see my sis-ter suffering. While I was getting stronger, Darla was getting weaker and her health quickly declined in a few months.

There was another sister, Violet who lived in the Black House but then moved into the sisters' house to help Darla. We both had to pre-pare the morphine bags for her. Darla was approaching hospice, yet she was still helping out the ministry, still trying to work from home on her laptop. The saddest part is that she was still working and The Group kept asking her to send money to Ghana. Lulu was the most persistent and had no problem taking her last paychecks to the very end. The doctors finally told Darla that she could no longer work.

Violet began complaining about taking care of Darla. In her last weeks, Darla's disposition became angry and she lashed out at me and Violet over little things. I did not take offense because I knew it was because of her health deteriorating. However, Violet remained a loyal mole to Shirley and Kaarme—gossiping about everyone. It was heartbreaking to see Violet betray Darla by gossiping about her hav-ing a bad attitude. There was absolutely no compassion, no love, and no heart for another human being who was suffering on her death-bed. *How on earth can I be a part of this mess?*

Sadly, Darla died in September 2012. It was during this time, I made up my mind that I was going to leave The Group. I never re-alized the dichotomy between Darla and me, but now it resonates so clearly. There was a shift in the timing of our surgeries with her health declining and mine getting stronger. Darla's death was the trigger to get me out of The Group. Many years later, after hearing my story, I was told that Darla was the sacrifice. She opened the door for me to leave. She died so that I could be free. Thank God for my forever sister.

## THE FUNERAL

As fear left me, my eyes began to open. Darla died in September of 2012 and the funeral was just awful. Kaarme was unable to hold off on his evil talking and complaining and verbally attacked me as we were preparing at the funeral parlor. He was telling me off and just treated me like dirt while the sisters were urging me to be quiet. They saw the fear I used to have for him was waning. I chose not to rise up and argue with him for Darla's sake as I was in deep mourning for her at that time. But I really didn't see anyone else shed a tear. Instead, they used the Polycom equipment to have a face-to-face service with Daddy Leviathan and his band in Ghana and they sang a few songs.

Then Kaarme began to preach to the hills about how Darla held onto Daddy Leviathan's word up to her last breath and everyone praised God. Everyone testified how "Darla held onto Daddy Leviathan's words until he told her to let go!" The true story is that Leviathan told Darla she would be healed of her cancer and that she would live. So instead of allowing herself to die, she fought for a number of days in excruciating pain. The cancer had spread all the way into her bones and the morphine did not give her the comfort she needed. But she kept holding on to his word believing this false prophecy until finally, the last time Daddy Leviathan spoke with her over the phone, he told her to let go and she finally gave in and died.

The whole testimony was supposed to be this great thing, but it became clear to me he was a false prophet. At the end of the service, I burst into uncontrollable tears for Darla and I didn't care who saw me. The Group had happy faces and felt a great testimony was shared but my heart was so hurt and I missed my sister. I felt alone in my mourning amongst the fake applause and praises that went out that day. The Group always finds a way to praise their idol Daddy Leviathan in all situations and it was just an awful sight to see.

# CHAPTER 22

## HURRICANE SANDY

*"It often takes the darkness of a storm to show us the light of God's presence."*
**Tony Evans**

Like the scales that fell off of the blind man's eyes when Jesus healed him, the same happened to me when the Sandy Storm of 2012 hit New Jersey. Although Sandy is associated with much loss for many, that storm represents a time of the "Great Waters" of Cleansing for me. Right after Darla's funeral, Sandy storm hit and we had no gas or electricity. I was still living in Darla's house in Elizabeth, New Jersey. Everyone in The Group, except one brother who lived downstairs had moved out. So it was us, along with Darla's mother who had moved in a few years back, and Darla's brother who was visiting from Minnesota. Her brother attended the funeral and extended his stay for a few weeks to handle her affairs living at the house.

Our home in Elizabeth was very cold but the house in Newark was fine. Two members of The Group that moved out bought a home that was about 5-10 minutes away and their home was not hit either. They had perfect gas and electricity. No one from either house offered for me to stay at their home. I was also concerned about Darla's mother who was in her 80s and I was ashamed that no one contacted me to see how she or her son was doing. We just toughed out the storm together in a cold house and made the best of it.

Since the electricity was out, I would go to my car to charge my phone. During this cold week, I had some conversations with Daddy Leviathan. I wasn't traveling to Bible study in Newark during the Sandy storm week, so I had time to mourn Darla's death with her brother and mother and take a step back.

Right before Sandy, I had a conversation with Shirley regarding the things I told a few of the sisters about Leviathan using me. Shirley said, "So I heard some of the things you said about Daddy Leviathan."

"Well you know I do feel Daddy Leviathan used me but that was then and now I just want God. Everything is Ok and my heart is healed."

I guess Daddy Leviathan and Shirley were getting worried about my "soul" or my money donations since I was starting to go against the grain. He reached out to me and our first conversation was a repeat of my conversation with him during the summer. But this time I told him I didn't see scripturally where a husband would deny his wife of affection. I was again questioning the whole theory on the role of the "spiritual wife." My questions began in my heart when Betty, one of the members started praying with me after the Bible study incident with Kaarme back in August. She encouraged me to continue to pray the way I did that day.

I was starting to hear God for myself and I started to search the Scriptures. The more I searched, the more I began to realize that the whole theory of the spiritual wife goes against what the Bible says, which commands husbands to love their wives. I didn't even get into researching polygamy at this point. So I challenged him and asked him to enlighten me. He said "Well…I believe what I'm doing is right." This is the same response he gave me when The Bishop called him out a year previously. Hmm, not a good comeback! Then he offered for me to visit him in Ghana in December. He offered me to sing with the band at some venues and implied it would also be a romantic trip. I told him "Oh, well I need to pray on that before I give you an answer." I could feel the big lump in his throat. No one ever openly told him they need to pray for guidance because his words are supposedly straight from God! Nevertheless, we got off the phone amiably and I had a ray of hope that I could still have a positive friendship with Daddy Leviathan and put the past behind us. Forgiveness was hugely important to me and I did not want to corrupt myself with anger and toxicity towards him.

A couple of days later I called him. I wanted to tell him some good news that was happening in my life. But before I could say a word, he started telling me off. His anger was based on our previous conversation. As he began to holler fire and brimstone, the phone cut off! Although this was expected because of my having no wifi, low battery, and generally bad connections because of the Sandy Storm outages, I took this as a Divine occurrence. I never called him back because, alas, he was revealing his true colors! He had no Scriptures to come back with as a supposed teacher and prophet of God. All he could offer was his ugly anger, self-righteousness, and pride. So, whenever I think of the Sandy storm, it was a time of cleansing and revelation.

One morning, after about a week and a half of living in a cold house, I was standing at the coffee machine at work and my coworkers were talking about the storm. Unlike The Group members, everyone at work was checking in with each other and asking how everyone was doing. One person from the Quality Control laboratory walked over to me and asked me "How are you doing and how's the family holding up through all of this?"

"Well we haven't had electricity for over a week, and it's been really cold. But I'm ok." She looked at me and said "Well you can stay over at my house in my daughter's room. She is away at college." Right there at the coffee machine, I broke down and wept like a baby. I didn't have any control. I had been keeping it all in and dealing with the fact I felt no love from my "family" The Group. Yet here is a coworker that offers me dinner and a warm bed for a night. I graciously accepted her invitation.

Spending the night at a stranger's house and not letting the Elder, Shirley, know was a huge step for me! By this time I asked the members of The Group that lived close by to at least extend an offer for Darla's mother and brother to stay with them. They told me her mother chose not to leave the house. So I had no problem packing my overnight bag early that morning before I went to work with the intent of driving to my coworker's home right after work. I felt bold but quite nervous and afraid. They indoctrinated us with stories of being in danger if we venture out on our own because we won't have their "covering through prayer and their grace." I had to push through all of those thoughts that were etched into my mind.

When I arrived at work, my coworker was eager and kind, telling me "Come over and have dinner with us. Your room is ready, here's the address." After work, I got in my car and as I drove I was torn and afraid but at the same time, I just needed some refuge. When I arrived, I got to see a happily married couple and photos of their beautiful daughter. Come to find out, both of them were physics majors with Masters and PhDs from their native home in Poland. My coworker confided in me that she wished she could get a job in the field of physics, but no job openings had been available. We had a wonderful time as she baked fresh homemade bread, and cooked a beautiful healthy meal and we all talked physics.

They took me back to my College senior projects in plasma physics and space plasma physics and I shared the joys of that time. What a huge icebreaker! I had such a beautiful time with this lovely couple. I got to see that everyone's life is not miserable and everyone's marriage doesn't have to be a failed marriage. Failed marriages and infidelity were all I saw for 25 years. But when I saw this 20-plus years married couple, how faithful they were to each other and the fact that they weren't even religious people, I saw a pureness in the union of two people I had not seen in a long time, if ever. I got to see how beautiful it is for one man and one woman's faithful relationship not be tainted with outsiders trying to control them. It was not a big deal from their perspective to allow me to stay with them, but to me, it was one of the most pivotal engagements that helped me rid my fears and have hope for a better future.

As I lay down in their daughter's room, I prayed for them, blessed the house, and asked God to do something special towards them for being so kind to me. Two months later, my co-worker got a new job working as a physicist; her long-time desire came to pass! I truly thank God for answering my prayers for them! Ironically, the very next day after my wonderful night with them, the electricity came back on. Timing is everything!

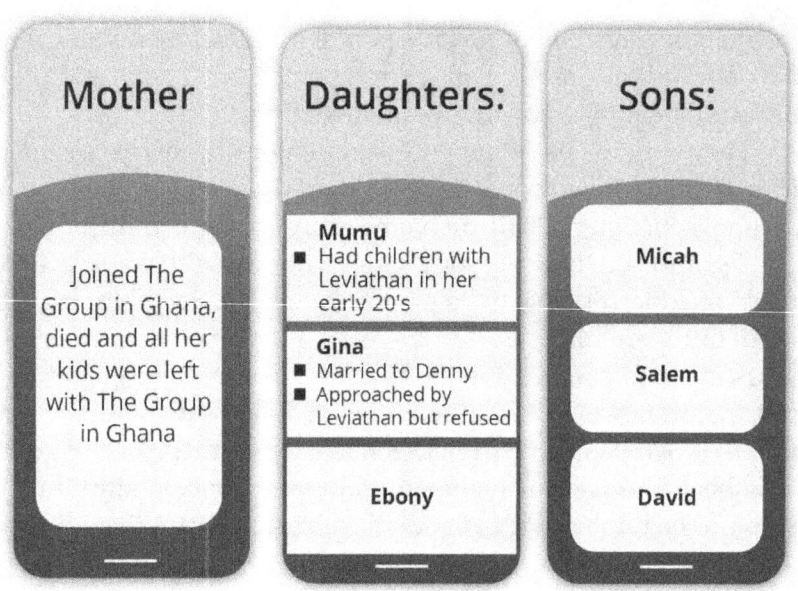

## American Family in Ghana
### The Davis Family

The Davis family has roots in Atlanta, but the mother traveled to Ghana on a few occasions and moved to Ghana with her six kids. After meeting The Group, she stayed with them but then died shortly, leaving the kids with The Group. I have spoken to Micah and included his interview in this project.

**Mother**

Joined The Group in Ghana, died and all her kids were left with The Group in Ghana

**Daughters:**

**Mumu**
- Had children with Leviathan in her early 20's

**Gina**
- Married to Denny
- Approached by Leviathan but refused

**Ebony**

**Sons:**

Micah

Salem

David

# CHAPTER 23

# BROTHERS BETRAYED

*"When I wanted to leave, they told me that I was going to die or fail in life because God would not be with me. I was young and scared. I did not want to be out of the will of God."*
**Micah**

I was fortunate to speak with other members of The Group who left. This is the story of Micah Davis. His story is different from others that I met in The Group. He was born in California and raised in Atlanta. During his early teenage years, his mother visited Ghana, West Africa, and she fell in love with the country. Micah's mom was tired of living in America and did not want her nine children growing up in a system designed for them to fail. In 1996, the opportunity for his mother and six of her children to move to Ghana became a reality when he was a pre-teen. Here is Micah's story in his own words:

*I first met The Group at an event where they were performing. They had talented dancers, musicians, and singers that knew how to capture a crowd. For the next year or so, I saw The Group perform many times at various venues. My oldest sister had joined them and lived on their compound by then.*

*A short time later, when I was 14 years old, my mother fell on hard times. She could no longer afford to take care of my siblings and me. Before that, my grandmother in Atlanta had been sending us money, but it was not enough to survive. My mother asked my sister about life in The Group. My sister told Mom about Daddy Leviathan fathering children with young girls, his many wives, and of his daily weed-smoking and beer-drinking. Overall, my sister seemed content, so my mother went to Daddy Leviathan and asked him if all of her children could live in the mansion and help in the ministry. She did not want us to struggle. My mom also wanted us to be around other American kids and learn the Bible. Daddy Leviathan agreed to take us in.*

*When we arrived, The Group threw us a welcoming party fit for royalty. There was tons of food, great music, dancing, and praises for our important step into the ministry family. Sadly, the jubilance wore off quickly. The first thing they did was separate us. We were not allowed to hang out or talk to each other. Elite members of The Group began concocting negative stories to make my siblings and me not like each other. My mom always told us to stick together in case anything happened to her, we could make it by having each other's back. This separation should have been my first red flag, but I was too young and naive to recognize the tactic.*

*I was grateful to be there and enjoyed Bible studies and learning God's Word. I took my studies seriously and became favored with Daddy Leviathan. As a teenager, there were so many beautiful girls in the compound. I and other boys my age would comment, "Wow she is beautiful." Immediately, we would be chastised by an older man who advised us that we should not make those types of comments because all of the young girls are for "the man of the house." When I heard this, I thought, Oh man, isn't he over 45? We're only 15! I decided not to worry about that dynamic since I was really grateful for food and a bed.*

*As one of the brothers of the house, I was a servant to Daddy Leviathan, his wives, and the women and children. I fetched water for the women to cook, washed dishes, cut grass with machetes, and did any required labor. After the food was prepared by the wives, me and the brothers ate last. There was a hierarchical order for everything. First Daddy Leviathan, the man of the house ate, then his wives, then his children, then the other women, and then the brothers. As time went on, food was scarce because many benefactors in America retired from their jobs, so they were on a smaller income, or they were sick or realized that their money was not going to a worthy cause. Me and other common servants were given two meals a day, often with no meat. It was usually rice with sauce or cabbage. Yet Daddy Leviathan and* his wives had full meals and always with meat. I was labeled ungrateful, a sinner, or the devil if I complained.

I really was so young and innocent. I looked up to Daddy Leviathan. I was grateful Daddy Leviathan was feeding me the word of God and providing for me. I was in awe that God talked to specifically to him! In my eyes, Daddy Leviathan was like a priest or bishop. I believed that Daddy Leviathan was the best thing that could have happened to my family. In my young mind, my mom did the right thing as there was no way Daddy Leviathan was going to do anything to harm us.

After being in The Group for a year, my mom died. Shortly thereafter, my dad died. My family in Atlanta sent letters to me and his siblings asking if we wanted to live with them in America. Unbeknownst to me, the Elders of The Group wrote nasty letters back to my family stating that we did not want to return to America and that The Group was their family. I remember how Daddy Leviathan and others quoted Scripture in Matthew 12:50, where the disciples told Jesus that his mother and brothers were waiting to speak with him, and Jesus said, "For whoever does the will of my Father in heaven is my brother and sister and mother." The Group was adamant about me and my siblings not having a relationship with our family. My family in Atlanta was deeply hurt after receiving those nasty letters.

When I got older, I became a member of the band. I sang, danced, and rapped. I used to get annoyed with Daddy Leviathan's mood swings. When the band set up for shows and began practicing, Daddy Leviathan would get upset and throw whatever was within his reach. He yelled at us like we were children. He always tried to make me and the brothers look bad to make himself look big. After a gig was over, the brothers had to carry all of the equipment and five-foot speakers back to the house. Regardless of when we got in at night, we were expected to complete all of our daily chores. I can say that me and the brothers were indentured servants for sure.

One afternoon the band was going to play music at a man's house. We were told by Daddy Leviathan that it was our job to clean the man's entire house before the show. Daddy Leviathan came in yelling and screaming because the bathroom was dirty. I finally started speaking up for myself since Daddy Leviathan had taken my voice and the voices of the brothers for too long. I told him that I was there to play music—not clean anyone's house. After Daddy Leviathan's outburst, I asked him outside to speak privately to him. I told Daddy Leviathan that I was not playing that gig. I felt so disrespected at that moment. Daddy Leviathan had disrespected the brothers too many times to count.

Later that evening, Daddy Leviathan called his henchwoman Shirley during Bible study and told her and everyone present that I had a demon in me. Daddy Leviathan was great at putting a person's business on display for judgment and ridicule from others. Even though countless times he would say, "If you don't feel like playing, then let me know, 'cause you don't have to. The people will know it's not coming from your heart." After that encounter, I spoke up and questioned Daddy Leviathan often around the house and in Bible study.

Every time I had the courage to speak to the Elders about leaving, they warned me that I would be ridiculed in America, held back in school, and made fun of because of my lack of education. I was homeschooled in The Group. I had no idea what grade level I should have been in. The Group also told me that I would end up dead if I didn't stay. They eventually convinced me that I needed them to live. They told me that I was going to fail in life because God was not going to be with me. All of their words scared me and I hung in there because I did not want to be laughed at by my peers, and I certainly did not want to be out of God's will.

Another task I had while in The Group was to watch the gate. I literally sat under a tree seven days a week for 15 years and watched the gate! I took turns with the brothers for two or three-hour shifts. The brothers were the security for the compound. He was fortunate that they were not robbed on my shift. Most of the robberies were inside jobs. Whenever new people came into The Group and Daddy Leviathan assigned them to house duties, thefts happened.

I believe that one of the main reasons why so many people stayed was because some of the things Daddy Leviathan prayed or prophesied about did come to pass. For example, he prayed for this large piece of land. They got the land. This land had three gold mines on it. However, it takes specialized equipment and expertise to mine the gold, so although Daddy Leviathan did not get rich from the mining, he wore gold on his entire body daily. Most of the gold came from the Americans in The Group, who put up money so he could buy it in Ghana.

Daddy Leviathan wore gold from head to toe. He literally had gold rings on all his fingers, toes, and neck, and on top of his head. He was treated like *a king at all times. Another time, Daddy Leviathan prayed for additional land, and they also got it. Although the land was in bad shape, it was something he could say he owned. The land did not have electricity or toilets. My brother stayed and worked on that land for years. My brother was loving and kind and did whatever was asked of him. When my brother finally wanted to leave, they called him the devil and other names. My brother never received as much as a "thank you" for his service.*

## Sexual Healing

*I knew all of Daddy Leviathan's wives and girls in Ghana. Daddy Leviathan had so many young girls and wives it was easy to lose count. He had children with his own nieces! He was married to sisters. He had sex with teenage girls regularly. I often saw Daddy Leviathan's nieces coming from his bedroom at 3 AM. There were orgies, and some of the younger wives did not like them. They wanted to have personal time with Daddy Leviathan. Anytime one of his wives would complain and threaten to leave him, he would throw a temper tantrum and act like he was going to leave the family. Then there would be a big outpouring begging him to stay. It was the same dramatic play every time.*

*Many of Daddy Leviathan's young wives would talk to the young men in The Group and relay what Daddy Leviathan was doing with them in the bedroom. They all shared that he was aggressive and not romantic. He forced them into sexual acts. He would often get the women high on weed while another woman was present in the room orchestrating the sex acts and telling the young women what to do to him. These sexual encounters happened in the same room where they prayed, had Bible study, and where the children were homeschooled.*

*I remember when a mother and father with four daughters brought them to Daddy Leviathan because they could not afford to care for them. They were hoping their daughters could receive an education. Two of the girls were not even teenagers. Daddy Leviathan wanted all four of them. One of the girls became pregnant, and the parents were furious. They told him not to have sex with their daughters. He continued with the sex acts, but made sure none of them became pregnant. Then there was another 14-year-old girl to whom Daddy Leviathan wrote letters. He wanted her badly. He begged her to come sit on his lap and spend time with him. He took her into the room and flashed a bright light into her vagina as if he were a gynecologist.*

171

*It was common for Daddy Leviathan to have three or four women and girls pregnant at the same time. I knew of everyone firsthand because it was my job to take them all to the hospital for delivery. There was no way Daddy Leviathan could go to the hospital after fathering so many children by children themselves. He was never involved in his children's lives. Instead, his children were passed off to other wives to look after if their mother was unable or needed a break.*

*I saw firsthand how all his women and girls would bicker and argue. They were jealous of each other. There were issues with who would bring Daddy Leviathan his food or who would sit next to him in the car. For most of the day, they were always jockeying for a position and time with him, except for one, Belle. She was an educated veterinarian who did not know what she was getting into. She married Daddy Leviathan and gave birth to a daughter. Once she realized what The Group was about in Ghana, she forbade him to ever touch her again. She was ostracized by the others and called crazy and the devil. She finally escaped to America, but only after many years.*

*There was a Bible study where I remember Daddy Leviathan spending an entire week on the topic, "You Don't Go Back on Your Promise." This message was directed to a young girl he wanted to have sex with. He promised her that she would be his last wife if she married him. She gave him a hard time and kept changing her mind. He was determined to have this young girl. His own daughters from his first wife in New Jersey told him that what he was doing was wrong. Daddy Leviathan told them to mind their business. He called them the devil. Everyone was the devil and a sinner except him!*

*The longer I was part of The Group I realized that Daddy Leviathan never had a positive vision from God. All he was doing was fulfilling his sexual fantasies with young girls. He took all of these young women from his own sons. When a young girl did not want to be with him, he had the Elders follow her around the house all day to ensure she was not talking to other guys her age. Daddy Leviathan is nothing more than a false, sex-crazed, evil, pedophile.*

## A Special Visitor

*Daddy Leviathan boasted for months about his spiritual father coming to Ghana for a visit. He showered The Bishop with praise for days. When The Bishop arrived, Daddy Leviathan put on a scene that was Oscar-worthy.*

*Daddy Leviathan ran downstairs and cried in The Bishop's lap. Bishop immediately noticed that the brothers were being misused and mistreated. But this show didn't last for long. The Bishop was staying in the second house, in another town away from the main house. Many of the brothers cleaved to the Bishop, and they wanted to be around him. Daddy Leviathan got jealous because of this. The brothers were finally getting manly advice from a man of God. The Bishop answered a lot of questions for the men, and he understood what was going on.*

*The Bishop confronted Daddy Leviathan and told him that it was wrong for him to take all these young women when you have all these young men around here. "Who are they supposed to be with?", he asked. Daddy Leviathan became defensive and made excuses for his actions. When The Bishop left, Daddy Leviathan told the brothers that The Bishop was jealous of him. After that, Daddy Leviathan continued to badmouth The Bishop and made sly comments like, "He ain't all that!"*

## Broke, Broken & Renewed

*As a young man, I needed money in my pocket. There were days when I kept asking myself, How could I be a man if I couldn't get a haircut or buy deodorant? Without money, I couldn't take care of myself. Daddy Leviathan frowned upon the brothers working unless it was to serve him. If any of the brothers worked, he said, "If you work, you are not spending time with God. If you work, then the people on your job will start rubbing off on you. That's why I don't want you to work!" He did not want anyone to work because he wanted to keep us separated from anyone who would see through The Group's false teachings. He knew he had to keep us secluded from the outside world.*

*With Daddy Leviathan, there was always double talk. He would never tell the members in America not to work. He needed their money to continue his lavish lifestyle and corrupt ministry. The only way I got money was when I went shopping with Daddy Leviathan's daughters or someone in the house, and I was told to keep the change. It would be one or two dollars. I used that money to put credits on his phone. Daddy Leviathan did not want anyone to have phones to call family.*

*Daddy Leviathan also played so many mind games. He would tell the brothers they could do something, and then when they did it, he became* enraged and would scream, "Who told you to do that?" He wanted to keep everyone in bondage, scared to make a move without his permission.

The more Daddy Leviathan made statements about work, I often wondered, what is the end game here? What are we doing? Waking up every day doing the same thing? I started rebelling. This time for real. I began questioning Daddy Leviathan in public and speaking my mind. I was a 28-year-old grown man living under Daddy Leviathan's corrupt rule. I was tired of this mess.

By now, Daddy Leviathan knew I was serious this time about leaving. One day a new pastor came to The Group. He became close with the congregation. This pastor saw things without anyone telling him. He knew that most of the men and women had gifts they were not using. There were members of The Group with Ivy League degrees. They were doctors, lawyers, scientists, and engineers. This angel of a pastor helped me with my passport. Then the pastor paid for my ticket to Atlanta. In 2018, I was finally free from Daddy Leviathan's rule at 29 years old. I had given The Group 15 years of my life!

I equate my experience in The Group to when the colonists came to Africa, and they gave the people Bibles, yet took everything from them. The Elders in The Group were never satisfied until they squeezed every ounce of a person's mind, body, and spirit out of him or her. If they saw you getting your stride back or gaining confidence in an area, they would knock you down harder than before.

Today, I am truly living my best life with my wife and daughter. I have a great job and recently bought a beautiful house with a two-car garage. I am living the life that God had predestined for me. Although I got sidetracked, my faith in God is renewed. My spirit of discernment is real! I pray that Daddy Leviathan and all of his henchwomen and henchmen get what they deserve.

I am free. I made up my mind that if anyone asked me about The Group, I would freely tell it. I will be blunt. I have no problem being public enemy number one. I am talking with everyone I can and talking with my family about my experience. My family in Atlanta is so happy to have me nearby to visit. Some of my family members are disappointed that they did not know what was happening and blamed themselves for not coming to bring my siblings and me home sooner.

I am so happy that many people I knew from The Group left. Even Daddy Leviathan's kids from his first legal marriage are no longer members. I think that so many former members of The Group need counseling. They need to know how a true man of God is supposed to treat people. Women need to be assured that sleeping with their uncle or sister's husband is wrong. There was so much negativity, evil, and condemnation that many members of The Group needed to decipher right from wrong. So many people were hurt by a twisted, corrupt predator. I hope all those who have escaped The Group heal and get the help they need.

As I stated, I gave The Group 15 years of my life. My sister had three children from Daddy Leviathan. Thankfully, she left as well. All of my brothers and sisters now live in Atlanta near each other. I am proud to say that we stayed together just like mama wanted. To God be the glory!

# CHAPTER 24

# A SISTER BETRAYED

*"Deceivers are the most dangerous members of society. They trifle with the best affections of our nature, and violate the most sacred obligations."*
**George Crabbe**

The following is an account of Theresa, a local Ghanaian. Theresa and I had a  good relationship while I was in The Group and after her departure. Here is her account in her own words.

*My name is Theresa. I was born and raised in Ghana. My path crossed with The Group in March 1998 when I was 20 years old. I was eager to model in a fashion show for the Ghanaian Independence Day celebration at the State House.*

*The guy who secured our modeling gig lost the spot where we were supposed to rehearse. Members of The Group's band were already there rehearsing. Someone approached us and offered us the opportunity to rehearse in the backyard of their house. Overall, everyone seemed nice, so they loaded nearly 70 of us in a big truck and drove to the purple house.*

*I hadn't heard anything about them before, but they were different. As a young woman who grew up in Ghana, we're used to a certain kind of clothes that displays confidence. They were decked out in African costumes. They looked nice, and I said to myself, "who do they think they are? How do they get off looking more African than me?" I thought.*

*Word got back to us that our event was canceled. So members of The Group told us that if we still wanted to model, we could do it during their set. Some of the models were not interested in performing with The Group since we were not being paid. As for me, I wanted to be a model and to be in the fashion industry, so even if it was without pay, I thought it would be a stepping stone to my career. So we started rehearsing in the house. Between that time of rehearsing, they started to share information about Africa and talk down to some of us, saying, "You are straightening your hair; you're looking white." A lot of the stuff they said made sense.*

*They brought in an interesting element to me; African history and Bible study. It was something that drew me to them. I had a background where my mother taught me about some African influences in the Bible, so I already knew about many people. Especially since we learned that civilization started in Africa. As someone interested in fashion and influencing the world, I was on board because I always wanted to come out with an African clothing collection.*

*I am somebody who likes to be different, and to me, they were very unique people. So I kept going to the purple house after that initial meeting. Then some time after, the Independence Day event, also known as Flags Day, arrived. It didn't quite turn out the way we planned. We didn't model for that occasion. Instead, we performed a choreographed dance, but we did not perform well. When we came back to the house after the performance, the Elders sat us down and had a meeting. They told us that we messed up, but that we looked good.*

*After a few months of engaging with The Group, there were only about ten modeling people left. Many people were not interested because the event already happened, so there was no incentive to hang around these people. There were Bible studies and African history studies, and just coming and spending time with our new Family was all they were offering. So as the numbers dwindled down, I was the **only one** left. I stayed because I became interested in the God factor.*

*I like to study and learn new things, so I visited the house every day during Bible study time. I felt like I needed to give my life to Christ again, but not in the "church" way. They would teach that the church as we know it today has failed. They boasted that the "church world" teaches folks about the Bible, but they don't live according to the Bible. They pointed to Scripture and gave us a tangible record of what they were saying that made sense.*

*So I was like, OK, maybe I can go this route instead of going to church. Then they shared about the big projects they wanted to do and the things that they wanted to do to impact the world. That was another thing that drew me. For example, they told us that if we were closer to the sea, then we would train the people to be fishermen, and the fishermen would have a place to store the fish, clean and smoke the fish, export fish, and make money. They also wanted to build community centers to help the local Ghanaians. So that's why I stayed.*

*There were also members of The Group with roots from Guyana, Haiti, and Kenya who also believed in what was promised. If there's one thing I know for sure, if The Group practiced what they said they believed, it would probably be the best thing that ever happened to the world. At the end of the day, they were saying to us, let's believe in ourselves. Let's produce what we eat. Let's eat well. Let's dress well. If we go back and look at our history, we were kings and queens. So what is wrong with believing that?*

*For years we were told that The Group acquired land and there were engineers drawing plans for the future buildings and communities that will be built from the wealth of mining activities. They boasted, "We will all be rich! We have land filled with gold!" But in reality, all of those plans fell through and never came to fruition.*

*I had plans to go to college for graphic design in the UK. My father, a banker, wanted me to go. I told him, "If all of us leave the country, who is going to build the country?" I regret saying that to him because I hurt his feelings. But at the time, I felt like somebody had to make sacrifices for the greater good of Ghana's future. I didn't go to college, but before making my decision, I ran my situation by the head of The Group, Daddy Leviathan. His answer was, "Well, it's up to you. You know how I feel about school. It's not that you can't go to school, it's that it's a different environment. You might forget some things and get caught up in the system of the world. So it's up to you."*

*Here was this leader figure telling a young 20-year-old woman the decision is up to me, yet on the other hand, he and other leaders were telling me to keep my loyalty to them. So I didn't go to college. I am not blaming The Group because I was old enough and smart enough to decide what I wanted to do. However, I do think that if I had a different outlook on my future prior to meeting them, I would have jumped on an offer to attend college. For most Africans, if you get an opportunity to study abroad, it improves a lot of things in your life.*

*I got a job at a printing press. I worked 8-5, and after that, I went to the purple house for Bible study. I had given my life to Christ. I was willing to go to the end of the earth to bring the Gospel. First, I was going every day. Then because the job I had didn't pay a lot, I started spending a lot of money* on transportation and I was falling short. The Elders had a conversation with me and told me that they could not give me transportation money every day. They told me to come every other day.

Then they moved further west, causing me to reduce my visits to the weekends. So after work on a Friday, I traveled to The Group via bus and remained with them until it was time to go to work on Monday morning. While I was there, I was either sewing costumes, helping to write a script for a play, helping with stage sets and props, drawing, or cooking. I didn't have a specific role per se, but wherever my skills were needed, I was there. Often they needed translators when they did performances and when they went to villages to teach, I would be the translator.

There were some people who were treated better than others when it came to the Elder's decision making. Initially, there was an agreement where they said they would give me a salary or payment. They also promised to account for me in their documentation of financial records whenever monies were given out. However, I never received actual pay.

## The Writing on The Wall

I briefly met Anna on one of her trips to Ghana. We were told that she was one of our biggest supporters. She was a person in the States who helped them financially or with whatever else that was needed. Anna and I became closer after I left The Group. By this time it was the year 2014 and I was 37 years old. I had been in The Group for 17 years. I don't have children and I don't have a husband. There's a certain status in life that is expected of Ghanaians. We are expected to have some type of aspiration. When I began to realize that I didn't have any aspirations and there was an overall lack of financial stability in my life (and in The Group) I felt something had to change. The following incidents of "Writing on The Wall" helped me make the final decision to leave The Group.

One day I needed sanitary napkins. I didn't have any money. I am from a family where my father was a banker, so we weren't poor and always had provision. However in The Group, there was a supply of different things in the house that would primarily go to preferred people and then if there were any leftovers the rest of us would get some supplies. I remember speaking to Shirley one day and asking, "Do you have some napkins? You know, girly supplies?"

"I don't have a lot," she replied. She literally opened one pack of sanitary napkins from the storehouse, took out four pads, and gave them to me. Standing there holding four pads was a sign of the handwriting on the wall. I knew I had to leave soon. It was a wake-up moment. When I am on my cycle, it lasts five days. Four pads weren't going to be enough.

I couldn't blame her because at this point I realized I had to start doing something for myself to make money. A short while later, I started making and selling soaps. Yet, at the same time, I couldn't do it outwardly because I did not want to give the impression that I was looking for other things outside of The Group or give the impression I was not happy with my current situation.

I felt like I was indispensable. I would do anything to help, and I would go everywhere to run errands for them in town. I didn't ask for much. I would sleep on a bench or a floor. It didn't matter if I only had a piece of bread or a bowl of rice for the entire day . I was fine. The Elders saw me as a soldier and I liked that because I was doing it all for the Gospel. I'm laughing because I see how stupid this sounds now.

I cut myself off from my family. But thank goodness they didn't give up on me. My mother died about nine months after I met The Group. Prior to this, they met my mom, and she initially liked them. Then someone got a hold of my mother and spoke the truth about them to her. One day I came in from Bible Study and my mother sat me down. She had this long list of women that were members of The Group who lived with Daddy Leviathan. She asked me who each one was. I was the most naive human being in the world. I said, "Oh, she's an engineer, and she plays the trumpet and saxophone. Oh, and her, she's the director of the programs." My mom said to me, "Do you know they are all his wives?"

At this point, I only knew of two wives and later on, I became aware of a third wife. When I met them for the first time, there was only one baby amongst them. At that time I was introduced to his first wife, Lela. But then there was this other young woman holding a baby who was calling Daddy Leviathan "Dada". I knew that in the Bible, Abraham and David had multiple wives. I am from Africa so it is not so strange to see one man married to a few women. However, my mother's list had nine women. I told her, "everyone is nice, they don't fight, and it's not toxic." My mother said, "But some of them are sisters."

"No, that's not true," I replied. Honestly, when I look back, I can't believe how stupid I was not to see what was happening around me. On my mother's deathbed, I promised I would stop going to The Group. Every day when I think of standing by her bedside and what course my life took after that, my heart breaks. After her death I continued to remain with The Group and I didn't see the manipulation until three or four years later. At that point when I would notice something, I remained silent because we were constantly taught to have a thankful heart and not complain about one another.

We focused on all of the Scriptures that taught us to be tolerant and to be understanding. Those were all of my favorites. So we were instructed not to murmur or complain. I had to tough it out. I couldn't share what I actually felt because I was programmed that it wasn't pleasing to God. I remember when my father warned me, "Don't go over there again. That man left America because he couldn't do the stuff here that he was doing over there. They are going to arrest him if he goes back." I don't know where my dad got that information from, but I still didn't see it. But now I believe he was right.

The Group talked about blood family and milk family. The Group is your blood family and should come first. Daddy Leviathan told a story of how he kicked his own son out of the house. The truth was that his son left because he found out his father was having sex with female members, and his son confronted him. They had an argument, and the son left.

It took a few incidents for me to leave. The dire financial conditions and not being appreciated were at the top of the list. I also realized I was becoming a very cynical person. I literally started questioning the existence of God. I remember being in a room and saying to myself, now I understand why these Atheists think there is no God.

No one was anointed to speak, except the Elders or someone considered Elite. As I sat for years amongst God's people reading the Bible and in prayer, I would get a word from God, but they were not going to let me speak. So that's the thing, it's like you could never be good enough. You could never be holy enough.

As time went on, I realized that I didn't even recognize myself. Who was the real Theresa? At that point I knew I had to leave. My initial plan was that I was going to still visit once in a while for Bible Study. I wanted to hear the word of God and I still believed they were the people of God, with the exception of some having messed up lives.

Now I had to figure out my exit plan because everybody that left The Group was demonized. Their names would come up in Bible study class and it was stressed that they were not of God anymore. I don't remember one person that left that house that was talked about in a positive light. The leaders would label them all as sinners. What's also funny to me is that they always casually said, "There's the gate. It's not locked. You can leave whenever you want." The truth is that when you leave, you become a public enemy. I decided I was going to leave on good terms and not burn any bridges.

It's hard to look back and remember how the Elder women gave the appearance of being content in their supposed "celibate lifestyle." Yet when Daddy Leviathan went after their daughters, they were OK with it. In reality he was sleeping with the Elders too, unbeknownst to the rest of The Group. I think often that these women have to be suffering internally. But will they leave? Probably never because they are loyal to Daddy Leviathan and so caught up in this mess that they don't think they can do anything else if they did leave.

The worst moments for me were the control, the manipulation, and the preferred people making me feel less of myself. It was demeaning. I literally felt like less of a person. That is what broke my spirit and helped in my decision to walk away. I think if I had been just a little bit appreciated, I probably would have still been there—still locked up in their negative, false world because I really believed in their vision to make Ghana a greater nation. My worst experience in life was making the wrong decision and allowing The Group to waste my time.

During my transitional days, I got a job as a virtual assistant. It was the one thing I could do without drawing a lot of attention to myself. When I started to make money, the wives in The Group started asking me for money. One day I got a call from Daddy's wife, Lela. She said one of his kids (from his younger wives) needed shoes. "You said you were going to send the money."

"Yes, I said once I got paid I will do it. I don't have it right now."

"When do you think you are going to get it?

"I don't know."

*I knew very well when I would get paid, but I was tired of the obligation. I didn't ask them to have all these children. Why should I feel forced to buy shoes for his child? I think she asked me again a week or so later, and I kept telling her I didn't have it, but I did. That day I went shopping, filled my refrigerator, and shut my door. That was one of the moments when I felt free. Although it took over 17 years, I was finally free.*

*I returned to the house and told close friends I was leaving. "I love you all, but I can't stay here." I spent my last night there and then in the morning I made my way to Daddy Leviathan's house because I respected him and wanted to tell him personally what my plans were. What I told him wasn't necessarily a lie.*

*"My family is really on me. They said they were going to send immigration after us. They are going to send the cops and stuff here. I don't want to start anything." As I'm saying this, tears are dripping down my face.*

*"Do they know about the teleconferencing and the awards?"*

*"At this point, they are so upset to the point where they actually think the reason why I don't come home, why I don't call, and the reason why I disconnected is that I am one of your wives."*

*"What?"*

*"Yes, somebody told them false information, so I need to go and prove to them that I can live without you guys. I have to prove that I am not being controlled. I am not being brainwashed."*

*"Alright. When do you leave?"*

*"The truck comes tomorrow, and I'm not coming back."*

*"OK." Daddy Leviathan called the other guys over. He also told me to let Lulu and Lela know. Within a few minutes, he had the whole band there, and he asked me what my favorite song was and they played it.*

*Then he opened up the Bible randomly, and wherever his eyes fell, he would read. He did that three times. If the message aligned it meant God was saying yes. I don't remember the specific scriptures he opened up to, but they were all about doing good deeds.*

*Then they brought him a dinner plate. They usually fed him a nice large portion. His plate had a full leg of chicken. He picked off a little bit and then passed the plate to me and said, "This is a blessing." Since I had already eaten, I took a little bite and passed it onto the next person. People came out waving and singing! They put on a big celebratory show.*

*After I left, it was confirmed by my best friend who was still with The Group what they really thought of me. She told me that the Elders informed everyone "just because everything is working well for her outside of the house, it doesn't mean God is blessing her." Someone else was told not to speak to me because "You don't know what spirit she's operating in." There were a lot of negative things I heard about me from other insiders. It hurt because even after I left and heard all the nasty stuff, I thought to myself, maybe I made a mistake. I was grasping for some kind of hope that these were good people who operated according to the Bible. Then I'd snap back and remember the underage girls, and Daddy's pedophilia.*

*The Elder women had concerns when I left. They called me to ask me whether I had told someone that a girl was pregnant by Daddy Leviathan. It was a young underage girl who I didn't even know was one of his wives. Why would I do that? If I wanted to get them in trouble, I would go to the police station or report them to immigration.*

*As I am looking at my life and trying to rebuild it, going after The Group would be a lifelong project and they are not worth any more of my time. Doing that would only imprison my soul and I want to leave everything about them behind me. I want to move on and live!*

# Part IV
# Metamorphosis
# Adult Butterfly:

*"For I know the plans I have for you declares the Lord, plans to prosper you and not harm you, plans to give you hope and a future… Jeremiah 29:11*

# CHAPTER 25

# A TRUE SPIRITUAL FATHER

*Keep on Praising God, He'll Give You Grace in the Hardest Place*
**-The Bishop**

I am forever thankful to God for bringing The Bishop into my life. God used The Bishop's love and wisdom to help me break away from The Group. He became the father figure that I needed my entire life. I'm grateful that I got to experience what it's like to have a spiritual father to protect and nourish me with the word of God, looking for nothing in return.

The Bishop was the Elder of The Group's Elders. He was supposedly highly regarded by Daddy Leviathan, Shirley, Lulu, and Lela. Most of us had never met him prior, but we heard about him through Shirley over the years from the late 1980s to the mid-2000s. He was like an icon that the Elders supposedly patterned themselves after. Daddy Leviathan would say that he was walking in the spirit of the Bishop and he imparted 10 years of his life to him. Then in the early 2000s, someone from The Group reached out to him, and just like that, we finally got to meet him! He made about three visits to Ghana and visited us at the Black House in Newark. We also made visits to him where his church was in upstate New York.

When The Bishop visited the Black House in Newark, and even when we went to visit him, I volunteered to do his manicures and pedicures. Doing natural pedicures was something I did for almost every member of The Group. I did not use nail polish. Instead, I soaked, cleaned, and buffed their rough feet and nails to a perfect shine. I've washed the feet of almost every member of The Group and it was something I loved and enjoyed for the entire span of years I was there. In the early days, I did manicures and pedicures for Leviathan, but it was short-lived. The chemistry between me and him was never right because he was so belittling towards me. I manicured Shirley's feet and hands on a regular basis. But again, our relationship was strained because I always knew at any time she could publicly ridicule me for her own selfish needs. However, when I introduced the Bishop to my natural manicures and pedicures, he would look at his nails in amazement, walking around showing everyone how shiny his nails were and bragging about me. During the treatments, we started to develop a father-daughter relationship. Since The Group always had imps around, those imps went back to the Elders to tell them of the rapport I had with the Bishop.

Bishop's last visit to the house was in 2011 and I remember it in detail to this day. After The Bishop arrived, I showed up at the Black House with my manicure and pedicure equipment like I always did. I saw Shirley and Kaarme talking and giving me dirty looks. Then Shirley came over to me and said I was forcing myself on him and discouraged me from even announcing that I was there to do his nails and feet. They were just blocking me from The Bishop's wisdom. Unbeknownst to me, they knew that the more time I spent with The Bishop, the wiser I would become to their tactics. But The Bishop called down to Shirley and asked "Where's Anna? I want my manicure and pedicure!" Shirley reluctantly told me The Bishop was asking for me. Bishop was staying in Shirley's room which was the largest and nicest in the house. We had plenty of privacy to discuss whatever Bishop wanted to share with me.

During our conversation, The Bishop told me that he did not agree with Leviathan's polygamous lifestyle and that he wrote Leviathan a letter stating his disagreement. He also witnessed how Daddy Leviathan treated the local Ghanaian children and adults that lived with them. He saw how they were treated like slaves and second-class citizens. During this conversation, he stated that Dr. Sherry, one of Daddy Leviathan's wives, told him that she wanted to have a baby.

She delivers all of Daddy Leviathan's babies in Ghana but she never bore him a child of her own. I remember Bishop raising his head with a stern voice saying, "Until she finds her own husband, she will not bear a child."

He went on to say anyone who is married to Leviathan is doomed since he is not operating in a Godly manner. His words cut deep into me because I was a "spiritual wife" and by then I already knew I still had issues with that anyway. I ended up calling Daddy Leviathan and told him what The Bishop said. His response was first weeping. He actually broke down over the phone. Then he said, "Well, I believe what I'm doing is right."

### Proverbs 12:15
*The way of a fool is right in his own eyes, but a wise man listens to counsel.*

After The Bishop left, a few months later Shirley was leading Bible Study as she always did and mentioned how Bishop is "suddenly" not agreeing with Daddy Leviathan's lifestyle. She mentioned he must be suffering from Alzheimer's because he agreed with it from the beginning. To me, this was the lowest moment of my being part of The Group. Prior to Bishop coming back into our lives, Shirley always held him high as the one who anointed her, Daddy Leviathan, Lulu, and Lela. She held him high as a prophet of God and warned us that he will know if we are not right with God and that he can see right through to who we really are. All these years of fear were instilled but when I finally met this humble man, my heart melted from all of the love that he had for all of us.

The interesting dichotomy is that when he entered back into our lives, he saw how the Elders were operating and saw through them all. He told me how they treat the native Ghanaians like slaves and he did not approve of pedophilia, adultery, and incestuous relations. He also performed a marriage ceremony for three sets of brides and grooms during one of his visits to Ghana, all children of the Elders. But after he left, Daddy Leviathan commanded that the newlyweds remain celibate. This lasted for two years. Shirley later lied and said

Bishop performed an engagement ceremony, even though she originally brought us the news with photos that it was a wedding. It was also clear to Bishop along with the brides and grooms that it was a wedding. When Bishop found this out, he was appalled that Daddy Leviathan held them from consummating their unions.

### 1Timothy4:1-3

*Now the Spirit speaketh expressly, that in the latter times some shall depart from the faith, giving heed to seducing spirits, and doctrines of devils; speaking lies in hypocrisy, having their own conscience seared with a hot iron, forbidding to marry…*

These along with other acts were abominable to the very core of Bishop's being and he chose not to ever set foot in Ghana or the Black House again. Shirley's played-off response was to defame him after all of the years she built him up, choosing Daddy Leviathan's lifestyle over the *Power of Truth*. Members of The Group drank the Kool-Aid and believed the lies that Shirley and Daddy Leviathan were forming about him. One member told me "Shirley said The Bishop doesn't believe in living free from sin." Her defamation of him worked, but not on me because we had already established a bond and I saw the pureness of his heart and intent.

After the Sandy Storm in 2012, a member who left The Group years prior, reached out to me to inform me that The Bishop was in town. By now, The Bishop had totally denounced The Group and didn't want his good name associated with them. The last time The Bishop visited Ghana he got very sick and something in his spirit told him to never go back again. I reached out to The Bishop to take him to his favorite restaurant, *Red Lobster* in Paramus, New Jersey.

I remember him looking at me from across the table after he enjoyed his wonderful meal of lobster and shrimp. He took his white napkin and dipped it in the water to wipe his mouth. He smiled and looked straight into my eyes and said, "I can see you are being torn in your spirit…."

"Bishop, I am considering leaving The Group. I don't want to support the lifestyle of their leader or the culture they created." The

Bishop said at first he did not believe Leviathan had multiple wives when he visited Ghana. "I thought all of those children running around belonged to The Group members. I can't believe they are all his children from so many young women!" The Bishop sat with me, prayed with me, and gave me comforting words. I confessed to him that I was one of the wives, albeit a "spiritual" wife, so I am at fault as well. "Anna, you are also a victim. Do not be ashamed. You were greatly deceived and now your eyes have been opened and you are doing the right thing."

After that dinner, The Bishop became my spiritual guide. I was in a safe space to offload all of my feelings. He was so supportive of me and from that day until his death, I spoke with Bishop on the phone just about every week. I was still afraid to leave, but The Bishop opened my eyes to the tactics of cult leaders. Fear was the main tactic to lead their congregation. I just needed peace and healing.

I was so tired of the drama but I was becoming mentally stronger. God showed me Daddy Leviathan's true colors and I already had revelations about wicked Shirley. At dinner that night with Bishop, without me mentioning her first, he said, "Shirley is a wicked woman." Hearing Bishop's confirmations about those in The Group strengthened me and gave me the courage to leave.

Now that Darla was gone, I was ready to break away from The Group. The Elders and others were trying to convince me to move into the Black House in Newark since Darla passed and no one knew what would become of her house in Elizabeth. I couldn't imagine living under the same roof as Kaarme. His toxic personality is not healthy for anyone. In my mind, I kept hearing, *why in the world would I work hard all day, get in the car to fight traffic for nearly two hours to live with people who hate me?*

I signed a lease for a one-bedroom apartment near my job. I still remember how nervous I was when I walked into the property management office. But God gave me the strength to move onward with my life. I was looking forward to new beginnings because it was two weeks before my birthday. So two days after my 48th birthday, I rented the smallest U-Haul available which was a 4x8 cargo trailer, and quietly moved out on a Saturday morning. I had such minimal belongings that there was still plenty of room in the trailer.

I started to feel guilty about leaving and told myself that I would continue to go to Bible study. I left on a Saturday and on Sunday morning someone from The Group called me because I didn't attend Bible study. Word got around that I was settling into my new place. Of course, The Elders and others talked about me like a dog. After hearing about the "saints" backbiting, there was no turning back from my decision to completely cut myself off from the toxicity. I was done. I felt a sigh of relief deep inside because I was never going to be in the presence of The Elders again.

## What Life I Have Left...

When I left The Group at the age of 48 years old I said to myself, *What life I have left, I want to preserve.* The scales of my eyes fell off and I saw The Group's organization for what they truly were: predators of young women for Daddy Leviathan to devour; predators of the young Ghanain men to be their house slaves; and predators of the US member's money, stripping them of their savings to support his hedonistic lifestyle. To know that to this day, they still have business sponsors supporting their educational program disturbs me. They get sponsored to support students in the US with students at their new headquarters in Accra, Ghana under the guise of good works. The dichotomy of supporting children and then exploiting and raping them is nothing new for The Group. These tactics were in place from the very beginning. They just put a new mask on it. So I ran far away from The Group and, since then, I never looked back. I'm certain they expected me to come back crawling, beat up by the world because they put fear in our minds about folks that leave. But I held onto my faith. I held onto the *Power of Truth* that comes from the Absolute Unadulterated Pure Power of God. I never expected to experience the great blessings of life that I've experienced and continue to enjoy to this day. I was just holding onto the last few breaths of life. Knowing that I gained my freedom despite the fact that I sacrificed so many years seemed like that was the great victory of my life. But I came to realize that I was embarking on a new wonderful beginning!

The first month in my apartment was surreal. I was getting the best sleep I ever had! I didn't have much furniture but The Bishop prayed with me over the phone, telling me that God will provide furniture for me. Lo and behold, a few weeks later the CEO of the company I was working for called me into his office and gave me a secret $30,000 bonus. He told me not to tell my boss and that he was happy with the work that I'd been doing. I was floored! I used the money to buy furniture and planned a detox cleanse trip with a group to Hawaii.

Then after exactly four weeks of being in the apartment, I felt deep in my spirit to write down my experiences. I fought against this because I prayed, "God I have forgiven them. I just want to move forward and put all of those experiences behind me. How can I expect to heal if I write down these horrible memories?" But the more I resisted, the more sleep left me. I was still afraid of The Group and the memory and pain of being with them was still very fresh. However, I knew that God was moving me to do this and I didn't understand it until many years later. All of those journal entries allowed me to publish this book. Sometimes we are led to do things we don't understand and in those times, we need to go with the flow!

## Snowy Day of Revelation

After I left, I had many questions about The Group, and The Bishop graciously answered them all. I had only been separated from The Group for about a month, so I was still conflicted in my spirit. *Was this the right thing to do?* I was so indoctrinated to believe that The Group was the greatest thing on the planet, and to break away from them would set My Life on a path of destruction. Although I was very happy and felt a huge burden lifted off my back, I wanted to know how the Elder's leadership came about.

I drove through a snowstorm to meet Bishop in Harlem, New York, on December 29, 2012. I was excited to see him since it was my first time in his presence since I packed my bags and moved out of the house in Elizabeth. I had my own apartment, and it was my first time living on my own. It was also the first time I surrounded myself with peace, quiet, and serenity. I walked into the room and saw Bishop with a long full beard dressed like a true prophet. Bishop was half Jewish and half Black. His head was covered with a black yarmulke. He dressed sharp, wearing a purple shirt and black slacks.

Bishop knew firsthand about abandonment and rejection. His Jewish father had a relationship with a Black woman and abandoned him as a child. He was able to use his negative experience to empower and help broken people like me. I sat at his feet for nearly two hours as he told me the story of The Group's beginnings which I depicted in the following organizational chart.

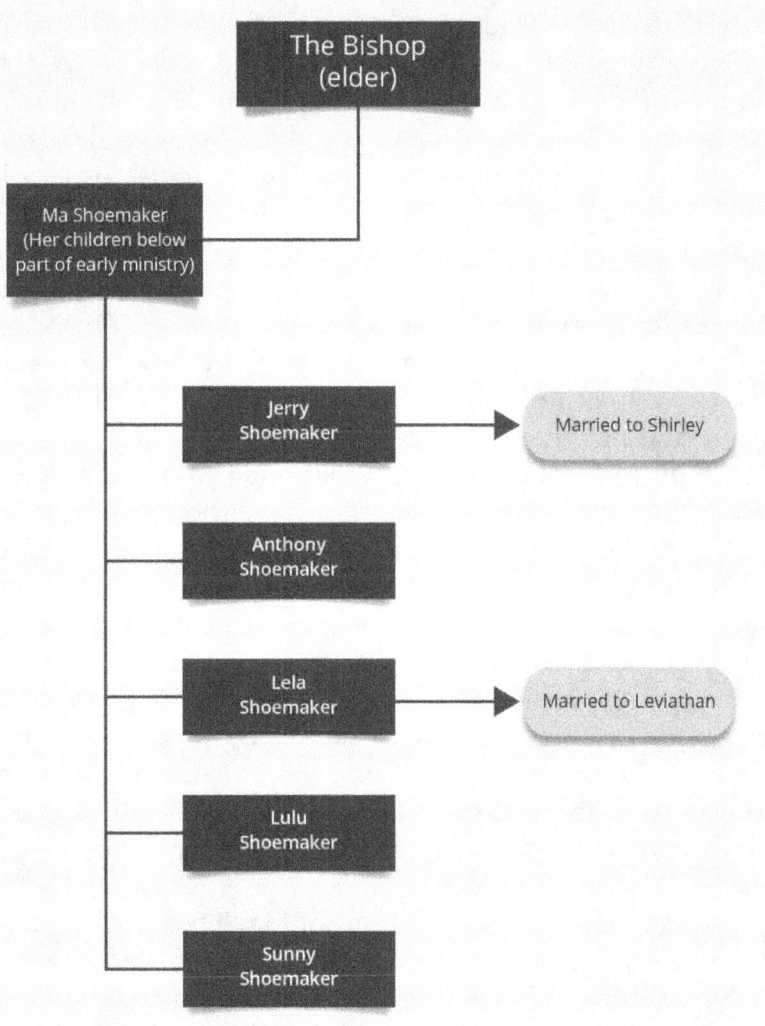

When I came into The Group they had already split from Ma Shoemaker, the well-respected Christian leader. One of the statements that the Elders always touted was that they obeyed their Elders. This was not true. If it were true, they would have obeyed Ma Shoemaker and never left a true ministry of love and compassion for others according to God's word.

Shirley would tell us that they were made out of a special mold after their Elders, Ma Shoemaker and The Bishop. She often stated that all of the Elders were obedient and did whatever they asked. At first, many of the Elders were really making an impact on people, and the ministry was thriving. Then Ma Shoemaker asked The Bishop to ordain her son Anthony and her son-in-law Daddy Leviathan. The Bishop said the church was too small to have two ordained ministers, and he felt that Anthony was ready to take the lead. The Bishop was willing to give Daddy Leviathan a ministry license, but not ordination. He did not feel moved to ordain Daddy Leviathan and back then he did not know why. Bishop stated that Ma Shoemaker was not happy with his decision to only ordain Anthony, so there was dissension. Ma Shoemaker split from The Bishop.

A short time after the split, The Group started a ministry at Montclair State University in Montclair, New Jersey. This brought in a large number of young college men and women. It was evident that Daddy Leviathan had a great gift of drawing in the youth through his charismatic preaching. There was one female student, Sherry, that Daddy Leviathan had his eye on. Daddy Leviathan moved Sherry into his home and she slept on a cot in the same bedroom with him and his wife. Ma Shoemaker told him that it was inappropriate to have another woman in his bedroom, but he paid her no mind. So much for obeying the Elders!

We were told that they split from Ma Shoemaker because of a disagreement in Scripture. Shirley always told us they never agreed on the topic of living free from sin, so this is why they split. Yet the true reason for the split was due to Daddy Leviathan's continuous sexual relationship with Sherry and eventually with other young women that were recruited from Montclair State University. Daddy Leviathan seduced these college women and they became disciples bringing in more women. Another reason for the split was that although Anthony was ordained, he was not as charismatic as Daddy Leviathan. There was resentment and jealousy, so Daddy Leviathan continued on his own path.

Hearing these stories and more from Bishop, let me know that I made the right decision to leave, albeit 25 years later.

# CHAPTER 26

# FREEDOM WINGS

When I left The Group in 2012 and for the next seven years, I was a single and free woman. I journaled my memories, thoughts, prayers, and dreams often. My career took off in an even greater direction, despite the cultural bias that exists with Black women in my field. I continued to move up the corporate ladder. I gave myself a lot of medical and holistic attention and repairs needed from the stress that affected my body. I sought to live a healthier lifestyle and kept my prayer life strong. Thankfully, I never experienced systemic fibroid growth after I left The Group and my doctor diagnosed that my uterus has returned to its normal size. A few years after I left I joined a local AME church that was led by a faithful husband and wife team. It was really important that I surrounded myself with positive examples of people that were not out to take advantage of me.

I bought a beautiful home in New Jersey near my job. When I first left, I was inclined to move on the other side of the country, away from everyone. But deep down inside I knew it was not time and I should not be driven by fear. Living in my first townhome was such a blessing since after 25 years, it was never something that I thought could be achieved. We were required to live with each other under one or two roofs. What a relief to live in peace!

During this time, I did feel lonely and I prayed for God to send me a husband. I felt cheated out of my childbearing years and I was hurting from being cheated out of having a loving partnership through marriage. Then in 2017, I made a declaration that I would no longer pray for a partner. By this time, I was happy with my life. I had traveled to Israel, Croatia, Ireland, and Germany. When I visited my job's headquarters in Israel, I stayed with a coworker who became like a sister to me. She took me to the river Jordan and Yardenit where baptisms are commonly performed. I got baptized and rededicated my life to God, with the intent of never pining for a partner again. That baptism put me in the state of *If God sends me a husband, that's great, but I'm prepared to be single for the rest of my life.* Besides, I was going to be 53 years young that year. I didn't want to spend another day being concerned about never marrying. I was finally content.

## PRELUDE TO MY BOAZ

One Saturday, I got a phone call from my brother that my mom fell and broke her hip. I left church early and drove to Long Island. Mom was in her late 80s so surgery was a big risk, but we had no choice. I stayed in Long Island for a week, waiting for her surgery to take place. The doctors kept postponing it. Finally, on November 1st, 2017, Mom had surgery. Mom and her roommate who was suffering from cancer, hit it off well. Even though Mom was loaded up with morphine, she started singing. My mom and her roommate sang songs thanking God for a successful surgery. I was relieved. We were all smiling and making small talk.

By then I was exhausted and ready to head back home to New Jersey for a few days. But Mom's roommate looked at me and said, "You need to stay one more day." When she said that to me, I literally felt a chill go down my spine. I knew it was God talking to me. I stopped making excuses for myself in my head as I felt that God was speaking to me through Mom's roommate. If I had driven home that night, I do not know how my life would have been because that next morning was life-changing.

*Love Is In the Air*

I went back to my mom's house for the night and got up early and went straight to the hospital. When I arrived, the nurses were trying to wash my mom, but she was in a lot of pain and they had difficulty handling her. I felt helpless because I could only sit there and watch as my mom cried out in pain. The nurses needed extra help. In the meantime, a young man was pacing outside the room, waiting to take my mother's roommate to rehabilitation.

One of the nurses called out and said, "Chase, Chase, please come in here and help us out with Ms. Armstrong. My head popped up when I heard his name. It was like my heart jumped. As Chase walked past me and headed straight towards my mom to help, I felt there was something very familiar about him and I lasered my eyes on him trying to figure out who he was. Then I remembered. *This might be Chase from Farmingdale*, I thought to myself. He was born in London, and his parents are from Guyana and Grenada. I caught another glimpse of him. *He looks a little like Chase, but kind of young for his age*.

My mind went back to my Farmingdale College track days. He was friends with my boyfriend Clive. Back then, Chase was shorter than me and a little clumsy. He was a hard worker and practiced every day. He was one of the most determined competitors compared to the other guys on the team. I remembered Chase because of his kind and gentle spirit and how we all had fun traveling to and from track meets.

So as I'm pondering, he finished helping the nurses. As he walked past me, I couldn't help but ask, "Excuse me did you go to Farmingdale, and were you on the track team?" He turned and looked at me. We locked eyes. It was as if time stopped in that very moment. An entire century passed by.

"Anna?" he asked.

"Chase?" I replied.

We both hollered, raised our hands, and hugged each other! I said, "Wow, you look great!" Chase said, "You too!" It was the greatest reunion I ever had in my life. We hadn't seen each other since 1986, the year I graduated and went off to the Ivy League University. Chase went off to Dowling College in Long Island and then to the Navy.

The man standing before me was not the Chase of 1986. This man was filled out, buffed, and quite handsome. In my mind, I said *My, my, my, you have grown and filled out in all the right places*! I was immediately attracted to his calm and polite disposition and his handsome exterior.

"It was so great seeing you, Chase. I'll be back in a couple of days."

"Yeah. Your mom is going to rehab tomorrow. I'll be there and I'll come to find you."

The next time I saw him we made more small talk and exchanged numbers. We talked often and went to dinner whenever I came to visit Mom on the weekends. The relationship progressed as Chase wanted to offer some level of friendship knowing that I was going through a tough time after my mother's surgery. Thanksgiving was coming soon, so I invited him to my cousin's house in Queens for a big dinner. That was the night we first kissed. The next day was his birthday and we attended my cousin's After Thanksgiving Fish Fry. Then he introduced me to his beloved friends in Freeport, Long Island who were also celebrating his birthday. I still remember the joy of that time as we continued to bond and our relationship grew deeper. He also celebrated Christmas with me, my brother, and my mom at the rehabilitation center. We brought the Christmas dinner to Mom.

But then, out of the blue, we fell in love. Chase came when I wasn't looking. We bonded so quickly. It was as if our souls were locked together. Every spring I made an annual trip to upstate New York to visit The Bishop and his family. So in the spring of 2018, I brought Chase to meet The Bishop. Years prior, Bishop said he prayed that God would send me a loving partner so that I would experience true love in the place of all the pain I experienced. I made some bad decisions during those years, meeting people on dating websites and meeting men that were not ready for a serious relationship. I asked him one day, "Bishop, how will I know if I meet someone that he is for me?" Bishop said, "Anna, when you meet your husband-to-be, you will know deep down in your heart that he is the one." But since years had passed by, I had resolved just to be happy, and it left my mind. But then as Chase and I were dating, after two months in, I knew he was the one. The funny thing is that Chase knew as well. I think it scared him because it happened so gloriously fast. The moment Bishop and Chase met it was an instant father-son bond. He loved Bishop, and Bishop loved him.

I recall thinking that I always wanted to be married to someone who would keep me young. The saying, "Be careful what you ask for," holds true. Chase never stopped being athletic since we graduated from Farmingdale. God sent me an avid triathlete who is a Masters Swim Coach. Chase completed the Iron Man competition in 2006. In that competition, Chase swam 2.4 miles, cycled 112 miles, and then ran a full marathon, 26.2 miles within a certain time frame to be donned "Iron Man!"

A year prior to reuniting with Chase, I blew out my knee playing basketball and I was still in pain from the surgery. The Dr. said I had mild arthritis when they removed one-third of my meniscus. This was devastating because I could no longer go running. But Chase introduced me to his triathlete community and in the summer of 2018, I volunteered to help at triathlon events all over Long Island. What a fun summer we had! Volunteering helped me learn about the sport and I also assisted him when he was competing. He encouraged me to get a bike and initiated private swimming lessons with me. I could barely get from one end of the pool to the other, doggy paddling.

In April of 2021, I competed in my first mini-triathlon. Chase saw this in my future and he was patient with me. He introduced me to a new world of open-water swimming and cycling that was so amazing it rehabilitated my knee. I was now in the company of triathletes that were in their 60s, 70s, and 80s letting me know that if I choose this lifestyle, I can be fit for the rest of my life.

During that year, I was working for a company that had projects overseas. I also spoke at conferences as an expert in my field. In October of 2018, I spoke at a conference in Boston and I was scheduled to travel to Amsterdam for another conference. Chase had some time off, so we planned on meeting up in Amsterdam and I was to arrive a day later. During the convention in Boston, my colleague knew I was going to meet Chase in Amsterdam so she said, "Anna, I can handle the booth here for the rest of our trip. Why don't you leave a day early and go to Amsterdam so you can meet up with Chase earlier." Not only did I go a day early, but Chase missed his morning flight and we ended up being on the same plane! I should have known that was a sign of good things to come!

On October 27, 2018, Chase proposed to me in Amsterdam. You can't get any more romantic than that! I said "YES!" Bishop married us on May 12, 2019, at the beautiful Swan Club, in Roslyn, New York. It poured down rain all day. The rain was a sign that blessings were showering down. Blessings are given in the form of our souls making us stronger by learning each other and growing together. It was the most beautiful wedding I had ever attended. I thank God we got married at that time and didn't wait until 2020 because that was when COVID-19 surfaced and the world changed as we knew it.

One of the main reasons why I believe Chase and I were able to bond so quickly is because we knew each other from college 30 years ago. We were both still the same person at our core. We had the same soul. I knew when I first looked into his eyes in the hospital room I felt like I saw into his soul. I saw that he was one of the most gentle men I could have ever known. I had dealt with abusive men in college and in The Group, not only from Daddy Leviathan but the brothers who were verbally abusive as well.

In full transparency, I still have trust issues. I trust my husband, but I am learning to trust him even more. The more I trust Chase, the more I am able to let go of my past. Working on this book and rehashing negative memories caused me to build up a wall around me and there were times I just had to stop writing to strengthen and nurture the bond that God put between us. I strive for unconditional love and complete trust. This is the power of our union.

Chase and I have been married for four years now and looking back, I had no idea I would ever be able to do things that I can do now. Because of his training, I got medals in all of the competitions I participated in. The first was the mini-triathlon in 2021 where I swam 400 M in the pool, six miles on the bike, and a two-mile run. The next two were Aquabike competitions where I placed and got medals in my age group. The last one was a gold medal in October 2022 where I did an open water swim of 800M and a 13-mile cycle on a hilly course.

We survived COVID-19 as we had to hunker down and live with my mother and brother in Long Island before we moved into our current home together. Those were trying times, but we all stuck together as a family. My husband introduced me to his wonderful world of friends and his beautiful Carribean family. It's like therapy for me to learn how to love and trust people and to know that everyone is not out to get me.

I never saw being a wife as a possibility in my life. Especially to a man this wonderful. I can't explain the words for it, but I am so grateful. I'm so blessed. I'm so happy. I'm so healthy! I finally got to do the thing I wanted to do when I first left The Group. We relocated to the West Coast to work for one of the largest companies in the world. Even though I've experienced the greatest joy down in my spirit, I hear God saying, *Honey, you ain't seen nothing yet. I brought you back to Long Island, and now to the West Coast. I'm breaking you out of the chrysalis. You're a butterfly! There's more to come. There's so much more to come.*

# Epilogue

I n November 2019, The Bishop said he wanted to ordain me as a Reverend and made plans for the spring of 2020. I was shocked, yet honored. Being ordained was the furthest thing from my mind because I was never an active teacher while I was in The Group. Looking back, I can see how he prepared me for this. We talked weekly and he sent me letters filled with lessons. He made sure that it was clear to me through Scripture that the culture and lifestyle of The Group were outside of God's will. We spoke often on his thoughts, concerns, and prayers for Bella and all of those who were trapped in Ghana. His concerns and prayers became my prayers and I feel like I never missed a beat in my relationship with God.

Many who eventually leave The Group don't get counseling and end up with disruptive lives. But because I was getting personal one-on-one counseling that turned into lessons, Bishop was building up a new foundation so that I can experience a loving and happy relationship with God on my own. Not only that, I was able to share stories of how I was able to help others.

Chase and I did not see The Bishop during the early stages of the COVID-19 pandemic, so the plans for a 2020 spring ordination were postponed. However, The Bishop was able to find a church that would allow the ordination to take place during the winter of 2020. Sadly, Bishop suffered from pneumonia for the past few years during the peak of the upstate New York cold weather. He was in his early 80's by this time. Even though he was weak and just gotten over a major flu, he was determined to complete the ordination. Chase and I arrived in upstate, New York and drove through the snow arriving on my birthday, in November 2020. Two days later, we went to the ceremony at a local church wearing our masks. The Bishop ordained me as a Reverend and ordained Chase as a Deacon because he said I needed someone to back me in my ministry. During the ordination, Bishop asked me to help carry on his life's work for his nonprofit ministry that he and his wife were leading. I said, "Yes" as it was the least I could do to support all of the wonderful works that he founded. I had no idea that this would be the last time I would see him.

In January 2021, The Bishop caught pneumonia again, but this time he succumbed and passed away. Chase and I drove again to upstate New York through the storms to attend his funeral. It was the toughest time for us and I still miss him to this very day. The Bishop had been in ministry for 52 years and poured into the community that ended up naming a street after him. The Mayor even showed up to the funeral and announced that they created a day to officially honor him. The Bishop touched so many lives and I am honored that my husband and I were the last ones to be ordained before he was called home to be with the Lord. I will always have the highest respect and appreciation for The Bishop, the one who rescued me and helped set my life on a beautiful course with more to come to continue his legacy. He chose the name of this book "Power of Truth" and taught me that the truth is the most important thing to live by because its power will keep us pure. I know now that part of my ministry is to tell my story and offer people hope. I am no longer a victim, but a powerful Victor! This is just the beginning of me mounting up on my new butterfly wings. Stay tuned...

# My 12 Steps to Loving Me

1. Understand my roots of low self-esteem
2. Understand why I attracted abusive people to myself
3. Forgive my Father
4. Forgive my Mother
5. Forgive The Group
6. Forgive myself
7. Love myself unconditionally
8. Love others unconditionally
9. Surround myself with good people
10. Move on the fact that I deserve goodness in my life
11. Expect only good things to come my way
12. Speak the truth and live

# CULT TACTICS

After leaving The Group I began researching information on cults and listening to podcasts on survivor stories. I came across a psychologist, Dr. Steven Hassan who is a renowned cult expert. He has written several books and he has created tools to help people identify if they are in a cult. He created a chart, The Influence Continuum, which demonstrates how we are constantly influenced by people, ideas, and forces throughout our lives. Of course, some influences are healthy while others are harmful by instilling dependency or obedience to a person or group.

In addition, I was floored to read about Dr. Hassan's BITE Model as so many tactics were on point to my experiences with The Group. I emailed him and he gave me permission to print The Influence Continuum and the BITE Model charts. Thank you, Dr. Hassan, as you have helped me and I hope my story helps so many others find the courage to safely leave a cult and live a healthy, fulfilling life.

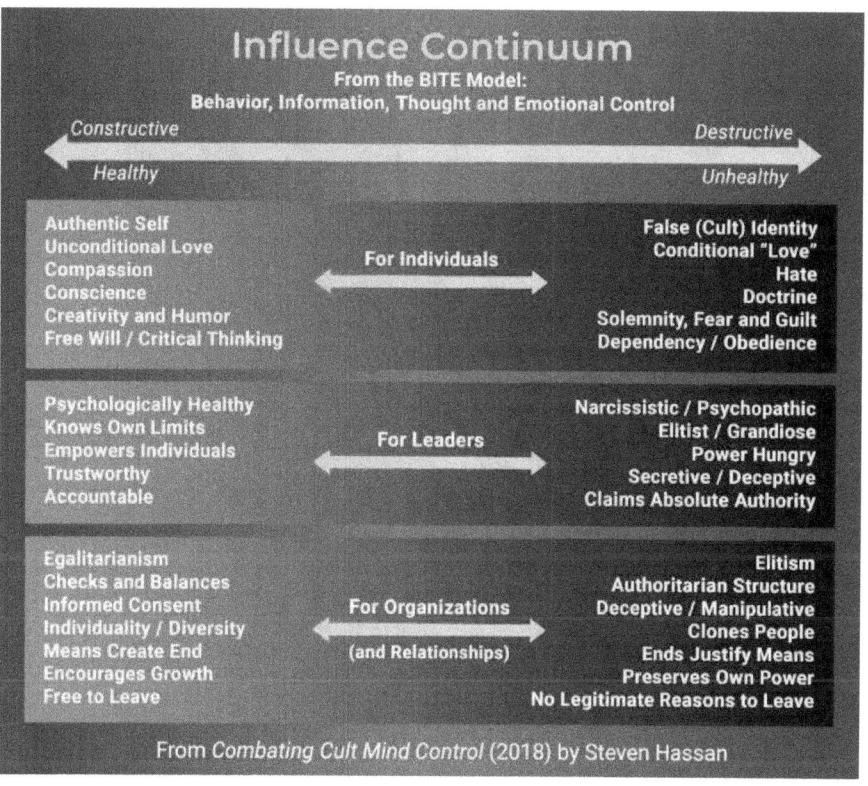

Used with permission

Model

Based on research and theory by Robert Jay Lifton, Margaret Singer, Edgar Schein, Louis Jolyon West, and others who studied brainwashing in Maoist China as well as cognitive dissonance theory by Leon Festinger, Steven Hassan developed the BITE Model to describe the specific methods that cults use to recruit and maintain control over people. "BITE" stands for Behavior, Information, Thought, and Emotional control.

## Behavior Control

1. Regulate individual's physical reality
2. Dictate where, how, and with whom the member lives and associates or isolates
3. When, how and with whom the member has sex
4. Control types of clothing and hairstyles
5. Regulate diet – food and drink, hunger and/or fasting
6. Manipulation and deprivation of sleep
7. Financial exploitation, manipulation or dependence
8. Restrict leisure, entertainment, vacation time
9. Major time spent with group indoctrination and rituals and/or self indoctrination including the Internet
10. Punish disobedience by beating, torture, burning, cutting, rape, or tattooing/branding
11. Rewards and punishments used to modify behaviors, both positive and negative
12. Discourage individualism, encourage group-think
13. Impose rigid rules and regulations
14. Permission required for major decisions
15. Threaten harm to family and friends
16. Force individual to rape or be raped
17. Encourage and engage in corporal punishment
18. Instill dependency and obedience
19. Kidnapping
20. Beating
21. Torture
22. Rape
23. Separation of Families
24. Imprisonment
25. Murder

## Information Control

 **Deception:**

    a. Deliberately withhold information

    b. Distort information to make it more acceptable

    c. Systematically lie to the cult member

 **Minimize or discourage access to non-cult sources of information, including:**

    a. Internet, TV, radio, books, articles, newspapers, magazines, media

    b. Critical information

    c. Former members

    d. Keep members busy so they don't have time to think and investigate

    e. Control through cell phone with texting, calls, internet tracking

 **Compartmentalize information into Outsider vs. Insider doctrines**

    a. Ensure that information is not freely accessible

    b. Control information at different levels and missions within group

    c. Allow only leadership to decide who needs to know what and when

 **Encourage spying on other members**

    a. Impose a buddy system to monitor and control member

    b. Report deviant thoughts, feelings and actions to leadership

    c. Ensure that individual behavior is monitored by group

 **Extensive use of cult-generated information and propaganda, including:**

    a. Newsletters, magazines, journals, audiotapes, videotapes, YouTube,

    b. Misquoting statements or using them out of context from non-cult
       sources movies and other media

 **Unethical use of confession**

    a. Information about sins used to disrupt and/or dissolve identity boundaries

    b. Withholding forgiveness or absolution

    c. Manipulation of memory, possible false memories

## Thought Control

1. **Require members to internalize the group's doctrine as truth**
   a. Adopting the group's 'map of reality' as reality
   b. Instill black and white thinking
   c. Decide between good vs. evil
   d. Organize people into us vs. them (insiders vs. outsiders)

2. **Change person's name and identity**

3. **Use of loaded language and clichés which constrict knowledge, stop critical thoughts and reduce complexities into platitudinous buzz words**

4. **Encourage only 'good and proper' thoughts**

5. **Hypnotic techniques are used to alter mental states, undermine critical thinking and even to age regress the member**

6. **Memories are manipulated and false memories are created**

7. **Teaching thought-stopping techniques which shut down reality testing by stopping negative thoughts and allowing only positive thoughts, including:**
   a. Denial, rationalization, justification, wishful thinking
   b. Chanting
   c. Meditating
   d. Praying
   e. Speaking in tongues
   f. Singing or humming

8. **Rejection of rational analysis, critical thinking, constructive criticism**

9. **Forbid critical questions about leader, doctrine, or policy allowed**

10. **Labeling alternative belief systems as illegitimate, evil, or not useful**

11. **Instill new "map of reality"**

## Emotional Control

 1. Manipulate and narrow the range of feelings – some emotions and/or needs are deemed as evil, wrong or selfish

 2. Teach emotion-stopping techniques to block feelings of homesickness, anger, doubt

 3. Make the person feel that problems are always their own fault, never the leader's or the group's fault

 4. Promote feelings of guilt or unworthiness, such as:
    a. Identity guilt
    b. You are not living up to your potential
    c. Your family is deficient
    d. Your past is suspect
    e. Your affiliations are unwise
    f. Your thoughts, feelings, actions are irrelevant or selfish
    g. Social guilt
    h. Historical guilt

 5. Instill fear, such as fear of:
    a. Thinking independently
    b. The outside world
    c. Enemies
    d. Losing one's salvation
    e. Leaving or being shunned by the group
    f. Other's disapproval
    g. Historical guilt

 6. Extremes of emotional highs and lows – love bombing and praise one moment and then declaring you are horrible sinner

 7. Ritualistic and sometimes public confession of sins

 8. Phobia indoctrination: inculcating irrational fears about leaving the group or questioning the leader's authority
    a. No happiness or fulfillment possible outside of the group
    b. Terrible consequences if you leave: hell, demon possession, incurable diseases, accidents, suicide, insanity, 10,000 reincarnations, etc.
    c. Shunning of those who leave; fear of being rejected by friends and family
    d. Never a legitimate reason to leave; those who leave are weak, undisciplined, unspiritual, worldly, brainwashed by family or counselor, or seduced by money, sex, or rock and roll
    e. Threats of harm to ex-member and family

BITE Model charts reprinted and used with permission.

"I HAVE A DUTY TO SPEAK THE TRUTH AS I SEE IT, AND SHARE NOT JUST MY TRIUMPHS, NOT JUST THE THINGS THAT FELT GOOD, BUT THE PAIN. THE INTENSE, OFTEN UNMITIGATED PAIN. IT IS IMPORTANT TO SHARE HOW I KNOW SURVIVAL IS SURVIVAL AND NOT JUST A WALK IN THE RAIN."

AUDRE LORDE

# About the Author

Anna Armstrong is a lover of science, music, and the arts. After completing her studies at an Ivy League University, she went on to a successful 30-year career in leadership roles at Fortune 100 companies. While Anna is currently pursuing her entrepreneurial dreams, she also loves to spend time taking walks, gardening, and enjoying outdoor activities and sports. Anna is known for her great sense of humor and her caring heart for others. Anna is forming a Power of Truth Foundation to help others who have suffered cult abuse. Go to poweroftruthbook.com for more information.

www.ingramcontent.com/pod-product-compliance
Lightning Source LLC
Chambersburg PA
CBHW060919120626
46553CB00001B/375